Dream Fights

- Great Boxing Matches Which Never Happened

Sam Dalton

Contents

INTRODUCTION

The book that follows is not a time machine parade of fantasy fights which pit the likes of Jack Johnson against Tyson Fury or Sugar Ray Robinson against his decades later namesake Sugar Ray Leonard. Such mythical fights are fun to debate but tough to realistically speculate on because in many cases the fighters fought in eras separated by so many decades they are almost impossible to compare. How do you compare someone like Gene Tunney to Lennox Lewis? You can't really.

This book is instead all about dream fights between fighters who fought in the SAME era. The fights that follow (with the exception of our battle between the Klitschko brothers - a fight their mother would never have sanctioned!) COULD have happened and in many cases SHOULD have happened but for some reason or other (boxing politics is unsurprisingly the main culprit in many cases) simply failed to transpire. Sometimes a big fight just doesn't get made and so forever becomes a 'what if?' scenario for boxing fans.

So, let's take a trawl through some of the fascinating fights which could conceivably have happened but never did. There are certainly some obvious ones here which we'll cover - like Lennox Lewis versus Riddick Bowe (the most intriguing heavyweight fight of the 1990s but one that shamefully never happened) and Big George Foreman v Mike Tyson in the early 1990s. Who wouldn't have loved to see Foreman v Tyson?

We'll also consider what might have happened if Sugar Ray Leonard had fought Aaron Pryor and Marvin Hagler had fought the great Wilfred Benitez. We'll shall also delve further back in time and speculate on what would have happened if Jack Dempsey had fought Harry Wills and how Rocky Marciano would have fared if he'd delayed his retirement to fight the young challenger named Floyd Patterson.

There's plenty more besides this in the book. We'll also discuss what might have happened if Britain's domestic legends Nigel Benn and Chris Eubank had tangled with - respectively - the American superstars Roy Jones Jr and

James Toney and we'll also take a look at the proposed late 1990s/early 2000s fight between Prince Naseem Hamed and Floyd Mayweather Jr which Bob Arum tried to make. We'll also consider what might have happened if Muhammad Ali had fought the Cuban Olympic legend Teófilo Stevenson in the 1970s. All this and much much more awaits in Dream Fights - Great Boxing Matches Which Never Happened...

ROBERTO DURAN
V
ALEXIS ARGUELLO

Roberto Duran is one of the most revered and popular fighters in boxing history. The Panamanian icon established himself as one of the greatest lightweight champions of all time in the seventies and then jumped two weight divisions to become the first man to beat Sugar Ray Leonard. He won world championships in four different weights and tangled with the likes of Leonard, Hearns, Hagler, Palomino, Benitez, Cuevas, Buchanan, and Barkley. When he fought the whole of Panama held its breath. Duran's relationship to Panama was a source of pride and motivation but also a burden. Today though Panama still reveres Duran and even put him on their stamps!

The young Duran grew up on these streets and was a sort of juvenile hustler, doing little dead end jobs and getting into trouble. He was born in the Panama Canal Zone, his father an American soldier (who he never really got to know) and his mother a pretty local girl from whom he inherited his dark good looks. Roberto was full of energy and always hungry. Food was scarce in the Duran house and the young Roberto would spend most of the day looking for a relative or friend who could supply a meal.

The hunger explains the fury of the young Duran in the ring, his desperation to escape the poverty of his youth and help his family. It also explains his later battles with his weight and inability to curb his spending habits. He had reckless eating and drinking habits during stages of his boxing career. Duran never forgot where he came from and this was both a weakness and a strength. He began fighting in the street and his natural strength and ferocity soon led to the boxing ring. After a fight he would drink champagne and throw money around. He had female groupies turning up to his training sessions at the height of his fame.

You get the impression that it never really hit home to Duran that one day he would get older and the big fights - or boxing altogether - would no longer be there to wipe out the financial debts. Duran was always likeable though. He had a pet lion in Panama that he used to do impressions of and always did his best to help those who were less fortunate than himself. He was an uncomplicated man who did his best in the role of a national hero.

The ferocious young Roberto was in his prime tearing up the lightweight division and he was absolutely vicious. When Ray Lampkin was hospitalized after a 1975 bout with 'Hands Of Stone', Duran told the press that if he had trained properly Lampkin would be in the morgue rather than the hospital. The erudite and polished Sugar Ray Leonard was totally thrown off kilter by Duran's insults and coldness prior to their first fight. Duran's colourful and intense rivalries with Hispanic fighters like Esteban De Jesus are also legendary for any boxing fan.

The stereotypical Panamanian boxer was a silky smooth artist whereas Duran fought more in the style of the great Mexican champions. It explained why he had such broad appeal across different cultural groups and nationalities. Duran stopped the Scottish fighter Kenny Buchanan for the lightweight title in 1972 in a foul infested and unstoppable performance. Duran was considered to be all but unbeatable at 135 pounds. He was less effective when he got older and moved up in weight but he still had his moments - most famously the first fight with Sugar Ray Leonard.

The transition from the young vicious Roberto to the older Duran, now more reliant on guile, was interesting to follow. In 1983 at Madison Square Garden, Duran, now considered to be past it and his reputation and career at an all time low after the 'No Mas' rematch with Leonard, was thrown in against the young power punching New Yorker Davey Moore for the WBA Junior Middleweight Championship. Moore was psychologically affected when the crowd - who are in his backyard afterall - all chanted for Duran. Duran then destroyed Moore in the ring. He'd forgotten more about boxing than Moore would ever know. Duran is rightly regarded to be a legend and an icon.

Alexis Arguello was one of the greatest boxers of the seventies and eighties and won world titles in three different weight divisions. Nicaragua had never had a world champion before Arguello and when he beat Rubén Olivares to win the featherweight championship in 1974 he became an instant hero and icon for his country. It would be difficult to explain just what Arguello meant to Nicaraguans except to say that he was a cherished symbol of national pride, even serving as their flag bearer at the 2008 Olympics.

But Arguello was much more than just a boxer and proof that the old saying about nice people always finishing last was plain wrong. He became known as El Caballero del Ring (The Gentleman of the Ring) and was amongst the most loved and respected of boxers, especially by anyone who came into contact with him. No one ever had a bad word to say about Arguello and he famously always became great friends with all of his notable former opponents. A class act both inside the ring and - most importantly - out of it.

As former lightweight champion, the popular American boxer Ray ("Boom Boom") Mancini, who lost to Arguello in his first attempt to win the crown, said - "I will forever be appreciative of being so closely associated with such a gentleman and champion. I always say that when you look up the word 'champion' in the dictionary and read of its qualities - class, grace, and humility - you will see a picture of Alexis Arguello."

Arguello's life outside of the ring was (like many Latin American boxers) complicated by politics and far from easy. It was like a film script you couldn't make up at times. It was impossible for famous Nicaraguans not to get dragged into the complex and murky political vortex of their country and such was the case for Arguello. Supporters of the dictator Anastasio Somoza exploited Arguello's image for their own ends in the seventies and when the Sandinistas took control of the country one of the first things they did was seize the millionaire boxer's financial assets and properties. They declared that he was not welcome anymore and a shocked Arguello promptly took up arms in the jungle and aligned himself to the Contras.

Not to mention the fact that around this time he also challenged the brilliant American Aaron Pryor for the junior welterweight championship in an audacious bid to become the first boxer to win world championships in four different weight divisions. The furious fourteen rounds they shared is widely regarded to constitute the greatest fight of the decade. Arguello had drug and alcohol problems when he retired from boxing but managed to conquer his demons in a rehabilitation centre.

To the surprise of many, he eventually met with Sandinista leader Daniel Ortega and agreed to work with him for the "greater good" of Nicaragua. A political career began but in 2009 Arguello was found dead at the age of 57 from a gunshot wound to the chest in his home. An apparent suicide. But he seemed happy and healthy to all who had encountered him in his last weeks. There were whispers that Arguello was increasingly dismayed by his association with Ortega and was about to go public. Was he murdered?

Arguello was part of that great pantheon of Latin American boxers of the eighties alongside such hallowed names as Wilfredo Gomez and Salvador Sanchez. Arguello was a darkly handsome somewhat distinguished looking tall spindly man who always seemed to be smiling in photographs taken of him outside the ring. Although politically naive he was intelligent and articulate and one of the hardest punching pound for pound boxers of all time, a trait that led to him being tagged El Flaco Explosivo - The Explosive Thin Man.

Arguello was not your stereotypical Latin boxer. He had a stand-up European style and was famous for his great patience. Arguello would rarely waste a punch and could be outboxed (for he was never the most fleet of foot) as he calmly stalked his opponents. But when he landed his patented right-cross it usually resulted in a spectacular knockout and there was no dog in Arguello whatsoever. If you beat him you would have to do it the hard way and engage in the battle of your life.

One of the extraordinary things about Arguello was that he lost his professional debut yet still became one of the greatest lighter weight boxers of the modern era. By the time he challenged Pyror in 1983 for his fourth world title his record was something like 80 wins and four defeats. Astonishing. You get world champions today who have only had 15 fights!

Arguello grew up in Managua's Barrio Monseñor Lezcano, a place so poor they would sometimes have to hunt Igaunas with slingshots so they had something for dinner. Boxing was Arguello's salvation from this life and he was always grateful for that. Arguello and Rubén Olivares fought each other to a standstill - both landing left hooks at the same time in the fateful thirteenth round. Arguello's was the one that did the damage. Arguello went to London and beat Jim Watt over fifteen rounds at Wembley Arena to win the lightweight title. It was his third world title and needless to say Watt became his friend afterwards and always spoke warmly of Arguello.

Arguello moved up to 140 pounds and challenged Pryor in a bid to become the first man to win world championships in four different weight divisions. Arguello was obsessed with making history but met his match in the unstable, erratic and wild Pyror, a human tornado who fought every round as if it was his last. Arguello hit Pryor with punches that would have levelled buildings but the American kept coming and stopped the Nicaraguan icon in the fourteenth round.

It became a controversial defeat though when television cameras and microphones picked up an incident late in the fight where Pryor's trainer Panama Lewis (a very dodgy character later banned for removing the padding from one of his fighter's gloves) rejected a water bottle from one of his assistants and asked for "the one I mixed" to give to Pryor instead. What was in the mysterious "black bottle"? We'll never know.

Lewis claimed it was soda water to settle Pryor's upset stomach but there are many theories about it being something more illegal. One popular theory is that Lewis had broken antihistamine pills into the water to give Pryor greater lung capacity. The shattered Arguello was devastated to lose. After so much success it was a bitter blow to swallow and he was deeply depressed. Arguello felt like he was drowning.

A rematch with Pryor and a couple of comebacks

followed and the Arguello story remained engrossing beyond the ring, not least because of the mystery surrounding his death. Arguello had become mayor of Managua but rumours were rife that the Sandinistas were going to discredit him. A gunshot wound to the chest is hardly consistent with suicide but it can't be ruled out. The most suspicious thing was that the investigation into his death was closed in 24 hours. Whatever the truth, Arguello joined the long list of boxers who died in mysterious circumstances.

A dream fight between Duran and Arguello was certainly floated in boxing circles in 1978. Arguello had won the 130 pound title and was now eyeing a jump to 135 to fight Duran. If anyone was capable of giving the fearsome Duran a good fight at this time it was surely Arguello. The publicity machine began to shift into gear and Duran was famously photographed aiming a clenched fist at a picture of Arguello. Sadly though, the fight didn't happen. Arguello had an off night and lost to Vilomar Fernandez while Duran decided to move up to welterweight - which left the 135 division clear for Arguello.

Arguello's camp still wanted the Duran fight but Duran was no longer interested and had bigger fish to fry in the form of Sugar Ray Leonard. So how would a fight between these two icons have potentially gone? The general consensus is that Duran would probably have proved to be strong for Arguello in the end and chopped him down for a late stoppage.

As we saw with the Aaron Pryor fight, Arguello could be somewhat negated by swarmers and high energy fighters who exerted constant pressure. Pryor's pressure that night though was almost supernatural. He fought for every minute of every round. Despite this it was still a give and take fight. Arguello frequently gave as good as he got that night.

Arguello was the epitome of calm under pressure. Even in the midst of an obstreperous brawl you could still see him thinking and adjusting, looking to get set so that he could land oe of those mighty punches which accounted for so many doomed opponents. Despite the perception that Duran is a heavy favourite in this dream fight, Arguello could not be completely counted out because Duran would have had to withstand some hellacious punches in order to exert his customary pressure and Arguello's right cross could put anyone to sleep if it landed properly.

The key to the fight would have been if Arguello could hurt Duran, or at least make him think twice about constantly steaming in to attack. If he couldn't put any dents in Duran and get some early respect then this fight could have turned into a very long and difficult night for Alexis. One thing is sure though - it would have been a great fight because Arguello would have thrown everything at Duran and fought his heart out. Even if Duran had won it wouldn't have been easy at all.

Arguello was a notoriously slow starter so Duran could be expected to take an early lead. This is the lightweight Duran and Duran at that weight was more aggressive than the counter punching Duran who later campaigned all the way up to middleweight. Duran was a good body puncher but Arguello was no slouch in that department either. One could expect some fierce exchanges in this fight once Arguello warmed up and got into his groove.

Arguello was somewhat easier to hit than Duran but he had a fairly reliable chin. It seems plausible that this fight could go the distance as both men had good stamina. Duran is likely to be busier and the stronger fighter but the rangy Arguello would not be an easy night for anyone - not even Roberto Duran. This fight would be a fast and furious brawl once it got going with plenty of two-way action. It's hard though to bet against the 135 pound version of Duran and the best guess is that he'd find a way to come out on top. What a fight this would have been had it happened.

ROCKY MARCIANO
V
FLOYD PATTERSON

Rocky Marciano was the world heavyweight boxing champion from 1952 to 1956 and the only heavyweight champion to ever remain unbeaten in his entire career (Marciano's final tally was 49 wins and no losses). He was born in 1923 in Brockton, Massachusetts under the name Rocco Francis Marchegiano and died in a plane crash in 1969 on the eve of his 46th birthday. His death was especially poignant because a surprise birthday celebration was awaiting him from his family and he'd just filmed a special (yet to be aired) for closed circuit cinemas where he shared the ring with Muhammad Ali acting out different scenarios for a computer to pick the winner of this mythical fantasy superfight.

Marciano's exact place in heavyweight history is still debated because he only made six defences (the great Joe Louis had made 25) but he is generally held up to be one of the ten greatest heavyweights of all time. More than anything Marciano is remembered as being one of the bravest and most determined men to ever step into a boxing ring. He was only 5'10 (short for a heavyweight, even in the 1950s) and looked like a fairly unimposing fellow in the flesh but he was ferocious, powerful, relentless and incredibly durable.

Marciano fought every round as if it was the last one and would batter arms and elbows - generally anything he could hit - with his clubbing blows until his opponent began to falter. He nearly always got cut badly and many of his most famous victories were achieved through a mask of blood. Marciano's legacy is perhaps best summed up by the reaction to a flippant comment (then heavyweight champion) Larry Holmes made about him in 1985. Holmes was 47-0 and closing in on Marciano's 49-0 record but he lost on a disputed decision to Michael Spinks and his dream of retiring undefeated and surpassing Marciano's career statistics were gone.

A bitter Holmes remarked after the fight that Rocky Marciano couldn't carry his jockstrap and so drew the wrath of boxing journalists and fans everywhere for his crass comment. Holmes later apologised and paid tribute to Marciano but the damage was done to his reputation. The essential difference between them was that Marciano would never have said anything like that about another boxer. He even cried after battering (a past it) Joe Louis in a 1951 bout because Louis had been one of his heroes.

AJ Liebling described the sight of the young raw Marciano as like "the understander in the nine-man pyramid of a troupe of Arab acrobats. He has big calves, forearms, wrists, and a neck so thick that it minimizes the span of his shoulders. He is neither tall nor heavy for a heavyweight, but gives the impression of bigness when you are close to him."

Boxing was murkier at the time of Marciano and shady mob connected characters like Frankie Carbo had a grip on the sport in America. Marciano's manager Al Weill was cooperative with mob characters and therefore Marciano had more opportunities. It was said that no title shot was awarded without Carbo's acquiescence.

If a new hotshot fighter arrived on the scene then one of Carbo's managers would look to assert some sort of ownership over said boxer. That was the system by which he maintained his controlling influence. It has been suggested that Marciano only got a disputed points win over Roland LaStarza in 1949 because of his manager's connections (not that Marciano himself knew what was going on).

Marciano was always a rather crude brawler who took three punches to land one. "I often looked over green kids who thought they could become fighters," Marciano's trainer Charley Goldman later reflected. "I'll eat my derby hat if I ever saw anyone cruder than Rocky. He was so awkward that we stood there and laughed. He didn't stand right. He didn't throw a punch right. He didn't block right. He didn't do anything right. Then he hit with a roundhouse right which nearly put a hole in someone's head, and I told Weill that maybe I could do something with him." Rocky's power, bravery and indomitable will to win made him formidable indeed.

Marciano won the heavyweight championship in 1952 against the classy Jersey Joe Walcott with a 13th round knockout. It was typical Marciano. He was behind on points and had a horrific cut on the bridge of his nose but nearly decapitated Walcott late in the fight when he finally connected with one of his patented right hands. Marciano didn't make many defences but he was good enough to beat Walcott and Ezzard Charles (both fine boxers) twice.

In 1955 after stopping the great (but by now very old) Archie Moore in nine rounds, Marciano did what very few boxers ever do. He walked away from the sport at the top of his game and never returned. There were rumours of a comeback a few times but - save for his 'computer superfight' with Ali - Marciano never entered the ring again. What was Marciano like in real life? Very down to earth and shy. He earned money from public appearances but found it daunting to speak even to a small group of people. He did a lot of charity work too.

He was perhaps most famous though amongst his friends for his attitude to money. Marciano was by all accounts notoriously careful - even tight - with his money, despite having earned millions. There are tales of him turning up to personal appearances in an old jacket with holes in it. Marciano is the one boxer who kept hold of every penny he made in the ring because spending money was never something to got used to or liked doing. This was because he had grown up on the breadline and knew what it was like to work for a living. He was terrified of ever being broke again.

Marciano competed in an era when boxing was second only to baseball in terms of popularity in the United States and so everyone had an opinion about it. He was in effect a real life Rocky Balboa of the fifties, slugging his way to improbable victories in the ring with his huge heart, becoming a great champion and popular celebrity through the media interest in him. Oh, and by the way, the computer said that Marciano would have knocked Ali out in the 13th round. "I got beat by a computer made by a white man in Alabama!" amusingly declared Ali after attending a screening of the computer fight.

Floyd Patterson was the world heavyweight boxing champion from 1956 to 1959 and again from 1960 to 1962. He won Gold at the 1952 Helsinki Olympics aged just 17 and when he beat Archie Moore in 1956 aged 21 he became the youngest world heavyweight champion in history. Patterson was also the first heavyweight champion to regain the title in the ring - a feat he accomplished by battering the happy-go-lucky Swede Ingemar Johansson in the second bout of their memorable trilogy in 1960. But Patterson was so plagued by self-doubt that writers dubbed him "Freud" Patterson.

"I think that within me, within every human being, there is a certain weakness," Patterson told the writer Gay Talese of Esquire magazine in 1964. "It is a weakness that exposes itself more when you're alone. And I have figured out that part of the reason I do the things I do, and cannot seem to conquer that one word 'myself' is because... is because I am a coward."

When Patterson lost his heavyweight championship to Sonny Liston he snuck out of his hotel after the fight alone wearing a fake beard and took a random flight to Madrid, wandering around the Spanish capital in disguise, too ashamed to show his face or return to America. The only thing he knew how to order in Spanish was soup so he had soup for dinner every night while he was there.

No heavyweight champion's political (Patterson was a black public figure in race torn sixties America and so could not avoid politics even if he'd tried) and historical stock ever shifted around with such rapidity. To this day no one can still quite decide if Patterson was a great fighter or merely a decent one but as a person - and perhaps even as a political symbol - there are few doubts that, in his own very eccentric way, he was a great man.

Patterson is a figure who unavoidably suffered from living in the shadow cast by Rocky Marciano and - later - Muhammad Ali. Patterson grew up as one of eleven children in the rough Bedford-Stuyvesant neighbourhood of Brooklyn. He was a petty thief and truant who often had a powerful yearning desire to escape from the world and be alone, riding lonely subway trains for hours. He hated that his parents had to work hard for such small reward and would steal fruit and milk to smuggle home.

The big turning point of his life came when he was sent to an upstate facility for troubled boys named Wiltwyck School at ten years old. He loved the fresh air and open spaces and - always shy, even later as an adult - began to come out of his shell in smaller classes. The young Patterson was also given boxing lessons and proved to be something of a natural.

When he returned to the city he went to a boxing club with his brothers and ended up at Gramercy Park Gym where he began a long association and friendship with manager/trainer Cus D'Amato. D'Amato was one of those grizzled Runyonesque characters who could only have existed in the world of boxing. He was considered to be a crank and a flake by many but the Nietzsche reading sage was an endlessly quotable eccentric and a man of independent integrity who was loved by his boxers. D'Amato told Patterson that fear and doubt was not only normal for a boxer but essential. "Fear is natural. Fear is your friend. When a deer walks through the forest it has fear. This is nature's way of keeping the deer alert. Without fear we would not survive."

D'Amato believed that the more you enjoyed life the more you feared death and so maintained a modest lifestyle. For D'Amato, money was only fit for "throwing off the back of trains." Decades later, when he was an old man near the end, D'Amato would discover another young teenage heavyweight prodigy in Mike Tyson. D'Amato adopted Tyson and, like Patterson, "Iron" Mike adored his wise mentor and hung on every word he uttered.

It is often said that if D'Amato had lived longer then Tyson would not have self-destructed the way he did. Certainly, Patterson never had anything but kind words to say about D'Amato and the influence the trainer had on him. He felt the adult Tyson had missed what he got from D'Amato. When Cus died, Tyson was still a teenager.

Though hardly similar physical types (one was lean and plausible while the other was like a cross between Joe Frazier and a tank) and separated by different decades and eras, both Patterson and Tyson fought with the "peek-a-boo" stance. Gloves up high as if glued around the face for protection and the elbows dug in against the ribs to guard against body blows. D'Amato trained his boxers to use the left-hook as the primary offensive weapon from this style but it did help of course that Patterson and Tyson both had remarkable handspeed for heavyweights.

D'Amato was cagey and shrewd in selecting opponents, looking for the least amount of risk to extend Floyd's time as champion. Patterson was knocked down more than any heavyweight champion in history and regarded to have a "glass jaw" but as Floyd himself pointed out, he nearly always got back up again to win the fight so his heart was never in question.

Patterson had memorable encounters with Johansson, a colourful Swede who spent more time chasing women than training but did have a very powerful right hand punch known as "Ingo's Bingo", and there was also the very strange match where Olympic champion Pete Rademacher challenged Floyd for the heavyweight championship of the world in his professional debut. This was more of an event (no surprise that the crafty Rademacher went on to become a successful businessman) than a fight but Rademacher did manage to knock Patterson down before his inevitable demise.

The problem for matchmaker D'Amato was that a new contender was rising rapidly in the rankings and couldn't be ignored for much longer. Charles "Sonny" Liston was the most chilling heavyweight to emerge for decades, perhaps ever. A hulking ex-convict with ham like fists and a surly demeanor, it was apparent to most that Liston would surely demolish the much smaller Patterson if they fought. D'Amato avoided the fight for as long as he could on the grounds that Liston was a nasty piece of work with criminal convictions but it was Patterson who insisted on taking the fight in the end. He'd been given a second chance himself and reasoned that he couldn't deny Sonny the same opportunity.

All of a sudden, Patterson, who America had been fairly ambivalent about, was now the public's darling, the hope of the "civilised" world. Liston was a scary looking former convict with mob connections. He was always in trouble. Drunk in public, speeding, disputes with the police, being sarcastic with reporters. No one wanted him to be heavyweight champion. Then there was Patterson. Humble, gentle disposition, quiet, intelligent, never in trouble. He even lived in a white neighbourhood. John F Kennedy met with Patterson and wished him luck. Eleanor Roosevelt was counting on him. The whole of liberal white America was counting on him. Most black folks were counting on him. And after two minutes in the ring with Liston the referee was counting on him, all the way to ten.

Although he was only 27 after his two (why anyone thought the rematch would be any different or was necessary is something of a mystery) first round losses to Liston, it looked to be the end for Floyd. He was written off as a poor champion who had taken advantage of a brief fallow period between the retirement of Rocky Marciano and the arrival of Liston. But Patterson proved the doubters wrong by fighting his way back to a title shot - this time against Liston's conqueror Muhammad Ali.

Ali may have become one of the most beloved people in the world but he was pretty much loathed by America in the sixties. Ali was seen as an irritating loudmouth and had become public enemy number one when he joined the Nation of Islam. Once again the unassuming Floyd had somehow become the standard bearer for "civilisation" and the establishment again, now confronting a man who belonged to a sinister organisation in the thrall of evil Svengali Malcom X. That was the general simplification.

To say that Patterson and Ali did not get on would be something of an understatement. Ali depicted Patterson as an anachronism, an Uncle Tom. A beneficiary of the sort of liberalism which approved the advancement of black people but only a certain kind - not the outspoken and brash types like Ali. For his part, Floyd was appalled by the separatist policy of the Nation of Islam and said Ali might as well have joined the KKK.

Patterson always insisted on non-segregated arenas at

his fights and had risked his life standing alongside Martin Luthor King at public meetings and speeches. He believed in civil rights and all people living together. To him, the Black Muslims were dangerous and weird. Patterson infuriated Ali by refusing to acknowledge his Muslim name, always referring to him as "Clay" instead. "That's the name his parents gave to him," he offered by way of explanation. It was one of the few times that Floyd had lacked class and Ali was determined to punish him.

Ali treated Patterson with utter disdain in the ring when they fought in 1965. Patterson had fast hands but the heavyweight division had never seen anyone as fast as Ali. The new champion picked apart Patterson with ease until the fight was stopped in the twelfth round. Patterson might have lost but he came out with a lot of credit for the way he stood up to the much bigger and faster Ali in the ring.

In the eyes of many, Patterson even deserved to win back a portion of the heavyweight title a few years later in 1968 but came away the victim of an unpopular majority decision in his fight with Jimmy Ellis for the vacant WBA title. Patterson fought on until 1972 (his last fight was actually a spirited rematch with Ali, Patterson being stopped on cuts in seven rounds) and posted a final record of 55 wins against eight losses. Despite staying in fighting shape for many years after, he never made a comeback out of respect for his second wife. It was time to give his family the attention he'd previously given to boxing.

In later years, Patterson became chairman of the New York State Athletic Commission for a time, campaigned to advance awareness and equality for HIV/Aids, worked as a counsellor, and also trained boxers. Patterson still somehow remains vaguely elusive after all these decades and several years after his death. He was clearly a fascinating character though and a very talented, dare we say underrated?, heavyweight champion.

So what would have happened if, rather than retiring, Marciano had stuck around to defend his title against Floyd Patterson? This would have been a classic experience versus youth fight and it is actually very difficult to predict who might have come out on top. Floyd was much faster than Marciano and would have used his speed and footwork to outbox Rocky early on. It seems more than likely that Rocky would - as usual - have got cut in this fight too. Rocky would have had to take a fair few punches from Floyd to get close enough to do some damage.

In terms of size, Floyd was a small heavyweight even for the 1960s so Rocky, who was small himself, would at least have not found himself outweighed to a preposterous degree.

One can easily conjure a scenario where Marciano, fighting through a veil of blood, would be behind on the cards after several rounds but still doggedly coming forward and starting to have more success with heavy shots to the body. The key to the fight is whether or not Rocky could have slowed Floyd down enough to mitigate Floyd's obvious advantages in speed and movement. Floyd would have the exuberance of youth on his side and as an unbeaten young challenger would be completely fearless.

Given that Marciano was a huge puncher and Floyd took many trips to the canvas in his career it seems plausible that Rocky might have stopped Patterson if he'd managed to land a really good punch. Floyd would probably have got up, as he was courageous and brave, but Rocky was a good finisher. If Floyd did go down or get into trouble in this fight it is hard to see how he could have survived. However, we should remember that Floyd could bang a bit too. If he began to land with regularity then he definitely could have hurt Rocky. Marciano clearly had a better chin than Floyd though so in the event of a knockout or stoppage it seems more likely that Rocky would be the victor in such a scenario.

The chances of this fight going the full fifteen rounds seem unlikely but not impossible. One would imagine that Floyd would win the majority of the rounds with his faster hands, busier punch rate, and nimble footwork, so in the event of a distance fight then Floyd would surely be the one with his hand raised at the final bell. Floyd had better reflexes and a better defence than Rocky so one would expect him to dominate many of the exchanges - especially early on.

Rocky would have been about 34 had he stayed around

to fight Floyd and it would not have been easy for him to catch up with such a fleet footed opponent. However, fighting someone quicker or more elusive than him was most assuredly not a new experience for Rocky! Marciano would doubtless have stalked Floyd patiently, more than willing to take clusters of punches in the hope of landing a blockbuster of his own. Marciano v Patterson is an intriguing fight because it is almost impossible to say what would have happened with any degree of certainty. It would have been a fascinating encounter full of ebbs and flows and be guaranteed to feature a few knockdowns.

JOE FRAZIER
V
KEN NORTON

Born in Beaufort, South Carolina, Joe Frazier endured a difficult childhood and eventually drifted to Philadelphia where he ended up working in a slaughterhouse cleaning blood from the floors. Legend has it that Sly Stallone took this part of the Frazier story and transplanted it to his film Rocky. Frazier grew strong and lean through hard work and his amateur career culminated in a Gold Medal at the 1964 Olympics. Frazier was a shortish (about 5'11) compact heavyweight who liked to work his way in and apply constant pressure to his opponent. His greatest weapon was his left-hook and he was a master at the art of bodypunching. Joe would never leave anything in the ring. He was as tough as they come and an all-action fighter.

Frazier was impressive when he turned professional and it was soon apparent that he had a bright future. He struggled though in his first big test when the rugged Oscar Bonavena had Frazier down twice in the second round. Joe escaped with a majority ten round decision (although he would fight a rematch a few years later and beat the Argentinian more convincingly this time). Frazier continued to learn his trade, beating names like Eddie Machen and George Chuvalo as he worked his way towards a title shot. In 1968 he beat Buster Mathis for the vacant NYSAC World heavyweight title. He then notched wins over names that included Jerry Quarry, Jimmy Ellis and Bob Foster, picking up the WBA and WBC belts along the way.

There could be no doubt that Joe was the true world heavyweight champion when he outscored Muhammad Ali (who was now finally able to box again after his ban for refusing the Vietnam draft) over 15 rounds in 1971 at Madison Square Garden in what remains arguably the most anticipated boxing match of all time. It was aptly dubbed The Fight of the Century. Frazier and Ali were eternal rivals and Ali's verbal jabs hurt the less articulate but intensely proud Joe. Ali tried to portray Frazier as some sort of establishment stooge (which was plainly ludicrous as Frazier's early life had been incredibly tough) and dubbed him "The Gorilla". Even in his later years in retirement, Frazier would refuse to shake Ali's hand at events and harbour a residual bitterness.

Frazier was probably at his peak around the time he fought Ali or possibly even in the late sixties. He knocked Ali down with a perfect left-hook in the last round to seal the decision win. Only someone with the chin and spirit of Ali could have got up from that punch after fighting fifteen punishing rounds. Frazier made two further defences of his championship before travelling to Kingston, Jamaica, to fight the undefeated George Foreman. Foreman was an Olympic champion too and known for his strength but he was also a big underdog. In a shocking upset, Frazier was stopped in the second round after several trips to the canvas. The fight was effectively over in the first round when Foreman staggered Frazier with a series of punches and dropped him with an uppercut. It was a brutal loss and one that must have been devastating for Joe.

After a points win over the British contender Joe Bugner, Frazier fought a non-title rematch with Ali in 1974. This time Ali boxed a more strategic and cunning fight and won a close decision. Joe regrouped with wins over Jerry Quarry and Jimmy Ellis and then fought the third of his trilogy with Ali in 1975 - the legendary Thrilla in Manila in the Philippines. Both men had slowed down a step or two by now and were clearly past their best and this - in addition to their tremendous pride - made it one of the most brutal fights in history. They fought in unbearable heat and neither man wanted to lose. Frazier, so puffed up around the face he could barely see, was pulled out at the end of the fourteenth round by his trainer Eddie Futch. It was a humane and correct act although Ali could barely stand up by this point and collapsed in the ring when he heard the fight was over.

The wear and tear of a punishing career had taken its

toll by now and Frazier fought just twice more. In 1976 he had a rematch with George Foreman and was stopped in the fifth round. In 1980 he made a comeback but a sluggish performance saw him maul his way to a messy draw with the unheralded Jumbo Cummings. Joe knew that his time was up and he never fought again. Frazier's place in history is sometimes underrated because of the way he lost his title to Foreman but we should remember that Foreman was an amazing heavyweight, so amazing he actually won the title again in the 1990s at the age of 45. Foreman's style was just all wrong for Joe. We shouldn't forget what an incredible fighter Joe was in his late sixties/early seventies prime. Not only was Frazier one of the most exciting heavyweights of all time he was - at his very best - one of the greatest.

Ken Norton fought Ali three times and always gave him trouble. Styles make fights and for some reason Ali could never quite work Norton out. Norton upset Ali in the early seventies. He was completely unknown but broke Ali's jaw early in the fight and won on points. Ali had fought most of the fight in excruciating pain but his sense of pride prevented him bailing out. Ali beat Norton in the return and then won a contentious decision in their third fight. Norton became disillusioned with boxing after that but like Leon Spinks was grateful to Ali because Ali had made him famous.

Ken Norton was a Marine before becoming a boxer and with his good looks and muscled physique got work as a model and actor. The part of Apollo Creed in Rocky was going to played by Norton but he pulled out two days before shooting began because of boxing commitments and was replaced by Carl Weathers. In the eighties, Norton was in a bad car smash that left him with slurred speech and ended his acting career. He still did an awful lot though. He was inducted into the Boxing Hall of Fame and winner of the Napoleon Hill Award for positive thinking. He was even twice voted "Father of the Year" by the Los Angeles Sentinel and the Los Angeles Times.

Norton picked up the vacant WBC title after outpointing Jimmy Young in 1977. He lost the title to Larry Holmes in 1978 in one of the greatest heavyweight fights of all time. The 15 round decision could have gone either way. Norton and

Holmes did not like each other at all and refused to yield any ground to one another for fifteen punishing rounds. Norton was an all action fighter with a cross armed defence. He liked to press forward and throw lots of punches. When he got into a groove he was very difficult to fight.

Though not a huge puncher (though Norton knockout victims Duane Bobick and Jerry Quarry may disagree with that assessment!), Norton was very strong with a good left hook. Ken Norton's kryptonite was big punchers. He was stopped early by George Foreman and Earnie Shavers. Norton only lasted 40 seconds with Gerry Cooney in 1981 but by that time he was well past his best. Frazier v Norton is one of the few big heavyweight fights that never got made in the 1970s. The reason for this? Well, it was simply because Frazier and Norton were good friends and so refused to fight one another. The pair did though spar many rounds together in camp.

It is always difficult to determine too much from sparring because sparring is not like a real fight under the lights but Eddie Futch, the legendary trainer, said that Joe could always handle Norton in sparring but by 1973 Norton was able to get the better of him because Joe had started to slip by then and was no longer in his absolute prime. Timing then could be everything in this fight. The prime Frazier would probably beat Norton but if this fight had been made between 1972 and 1975 then Norton would have had a very good chance at an upset.

The great thing about this fight is that there is no clear consensus on who would have won had they fought around 1972/1973. They match up very well. Both are strong and like to come forward and both threw a mean left hook. This would have been a bruiser of a fight with no quarter given. Joe was a fairly slow starter so one presumes that Norton might well have taken some of the early rounds by virtue of being busier.

The key to this fight though is what happens when Frazier begins to get his inside game going and land that potent left-hook (both upstairs and downstairs). An early knockout for either seems unlikely and it is very possible that this one might even have gone to the cards. the frustrating thing about this fight not being made is that it would have been highly entertaining. This is a bout that certainly wouldn't have lacked for action. Norton could certainly win if he built an early lead and managed to fight on level terms with Joe in the middle and championship rounds. Frazier would have to impose his will on Norton, bull him to the ropes, and be busier. If Frazier managed to do this then it is difficult to see how Norton could have come out on top. Frazier was no joke. Larry Holmes said he got his ribs broken when he sparred with Frazier in the early seventies.

The most plausible outcome is a late stoppage or close decision win for Frazier but it isn't a fight you would have wanted to put too much money on. Ken Norton, at his very best, would have been more than capable of giving Frazier a very difficult fight. This is a fight that Norton can win but logic dictates that Frazier probably would have found a way to grind out a win in what would undoubtedly have been a tough and action packed fight.

THOMAS HEARNS
V
MIKE McCALLUM

Thomas Hearns was one of the most popular, exciting and successful boxers of the modern era. He won several world titles in different weights and became one of the 'five kings' alongside Sugar Ray Leonard, Marvin Hagler, Roberto Duran and Wilfred Benitez - a clutch of great boxers who fought in a number of memorable bouts against one another and made up boxing's last golden age. Emanuel Steward was the famous trainer/manager who guided Hearns and also the founder of the legendary Kronk Gym in Detroit where the 'Hitman' was discovered and many champions emerged from in its glory days. The Kronk Gym was in the bowels of an old building, claustrophobic and unbearably hot from overhead pipes. Sparring sessions there were better than many real fights.

Hearns was originally supposed to meet his great nemesis Sugar Ray Leonard in 1978 when they were rising prospects but Leonard's shrewd trainer Angelo Dundee decided they should meet later in their careers when much more money would be at stake. Hearns then fought the fearsome Mexican legend Pipino Cuevas for the world welterweight championship in front of 11,000 people in Detroit's Joe Louis Arena. Hearns destroyed the iron-chinned Cuevas in two rounds.

Detroit had put the United States 'on wheels' after WW2 in the auto-boom but car production peaked in 1955 only to be followed by a recession that put twenty per cent of the workforce out of a job. Poor black migrants like the Hearns family then settled into areas that looked like warzones. When Hearns became a superstar boxer he gave the city something to be proud of again and even in the twilight of his career could still draw a big crowd in his home town.

Hearns lost his 1981 superfight with Sugar Ray Leonard

in the fourteenth round of a classic encounter. Hearns was also supposed to fight Marvin Hagler in 1982 in a deal that would see Hagler defend his title against three Kronk boxers culminating in Hearns. Their classic encounter would eventually occur in 1985. Hagler won in the third round of a brutal fight. Hagler was cut and on the verge of being stopped (due to the cut) when he stopped an exhausted Hearns.

Many believe that Hearns could have outboxed Hagler with his speed and footwork but Hearns said he had no legs that night and was forced to stand and slug it out. Hearns won world titles from welterweight to light-heavyweight. He beat the likes of Cuevas, Benitez, Roldan, and Shuler. Hearns also stopped the rock chinned Dennis Andries at light-heavyweight. The greatest performance of Hearns came when he stopped Roberto Duran in two rounds in 1984. This was a terrifying knockout.

In 1989, Hearns fought his old rival Sugar Leonard again and the result was a disputed draw that most felt Hearns had won. Both were past their best but Hearns still had his mighty punch. Hearns staged one last great twilight performance in 1991 when he outclassed the undefeated young light-heavyweight champion Virgil Hill. Hearns ended with a record of 61-5-1. At least two of those losses came when he was well past his best.

Hearns was a tall boxer with incredible handspeed and a devastating right cross. He was also a great body puncher too. Hearns could be vulnerable though if you tagged him. He didn't have the best chin. His chin was usually good enough though to buy him enough time to land his right hand. One other thing about Hearns too is that because he was super fast with a long reach he was almost impossible to outbox. If you wanted to beat Hearns you had to take the fight to him and rough him up - a strategy which would place in the danger zone of that legendary right hand. Hearns it appears lived to box - which explains why he found it so hard to retire.

Mike McCallum was born in Jamaica and moved to the United States to pursue a boxing career. McCallum was very unappreciated in the 1980s - much to his frustration. He yearned to fight the big names like Hagler, Duran, and Hearns but could never land any of these fights. He was a great boxer but he wasn't a big name or someone who was naturally charismatic. He was simply a brilliant ring technician and so more appreciated by purists than casual boxing fans. McCallum was part of the Kronk gym for a time and often sparred with Hearns.

Manny Steward said of McCallum - "The main thing that I remember about Mike is he's the most naturally gifted fighter that ever walked into my gym. He did everything effortlessly. I mean he was just so smooth, so automatic. You would show him a little trick, and well here's a good example. One day he was boxing with Tommy, and I said to him, 'I'm gonna show you a little trick. Tommy jabs with his left hand down, so I want you to parry it and step over real smooth, and shoot a little one, two and hit him on the chin.' He hit him three consecutive times, and finally Tommy stopped and said, 'How come I can't stop him from hitting me?' And everyone laughed! He did it so smooth-and I've shown that to a lot of fighters-but no one was ever able to do it, and he could hit anybody to the body! The workouts between Mike and Tommy were just unbelievable. They were better than most fights. They were just phenomenal!"

McCallum made several defences of the WBA junior-middlewight championship. Among his victims were Milton McCrory, Donald Curry, and the murderous punching Julian Jackson. McCallum was a spindly and crafty fighter known as The Body Snatcher because of his body punching skills. McCallum was usually a bit slow to get going but he was very difficult to outbox and incredibly strong and awkward. He would adjust to his opponent's style and nearly always get the job done. McCallum would just slowly impose his will on people and grind them down. The reason why he never got a big superfight is that he was seen as high risk and low reward. Despite his great talent, McCallum just wasn't a big name and didn't have much of a following. That's just the way it goes sometimes.

McCallum suffered his first loss at middleweight to the tricky Sumbu Kalambay but later beat Kalambay in a rematch. Mike won the WBA championship at middleweight and beat the likes of Herol Graham and Steve Collins at 160 pounds. He engaged in two classic bouts (there was later a third bout) with James Toney and although past his prime gave Toney all he could handle. McCallum, now in the veteran stage of his career, amazingly won the light-heavyweight championship from Jeff Harding in 1994. McCallum was definitely at his best though at 154 pounds. He is regarded to be one the greatest junior-middleweights in history.

So, what would have happened had McCallum and Hearns fought? They could have fought at 154 or 160 around the mid 1980s. The first instinct in this fight is to presume that Hearns would probably be a heavy favourite but that wouldn't necessarily be the case. McCallum would definitely be a live underdog in this fight. In fact, many believe he might have had the style and fortitude to be a stylistic nightmare for Tommy. If McCallum weathered the expected early blitz by Tommy then this potentially becomes a very interesting fight indeed.

The two men are evenly matched when it comes to dimensions as both had the same reach. Hearns usually enjoyed a reach advantage over his opponents but this wouldn't be the case with Mike. Hearns would definitely have an advantage when it came to handspeed but McCallum's timing might help negate this factor. Mike managed to get the better of faster opponents like Don Curry, Herol Graham, and Julian Jackson so speed wasn't something that unduly bothered him. McCallum would also be acclimatised to the speed of Hearns after sparring so many rounds with him.

Hearns also has an advantage when it comes to mobility and footwork. Tommy could get up on his toes and move when he wanted to. McCallum was a flat-footed type who would patiently stalk his opponents and cut off the ring. As far as boxing ability goes, they match up well. Hearns was a master boxer on the outside but McCallum was no slouch either. His fights with Toney were a masterclass for purists. In terms of punching power Hearns obviously has the edge. Tommy was a genuine knockout artist whereas Mike tended (his one punch kayo of Don Curry notwithstanding) to grind people down and slowly batter them into submission.

When it comes to durability and stamina one would definitely give McCallum the edge over Hearns. McCallum had a great chin whereas Tommy would usually wobble a bit if someone caught him with a really good punch. Hearns looked a trifle wobbly at times before he stopped Roldan to win his fourth title and he was stopped by Barkley in their first fight.

The key to this fight is the approach taken by Hearns. Tommy could outbox anyone in his prime. He outboxed Wilfred Benitez and was outboxing Sugar Ray Leonard in 1981 before he began to run out of gas. It was after the Duran fight where Tommy seemed to throw all caution to the wind and try and knock everyone out in the first round. After the Duran fight The Motor City Cobra was no more and Hearns just wanted to be The Hitman all the time.

Such a strategy would be risky against McCallum because if Mike weathered the early storm and Tommy punched himself out then it would turn into a very long and difficult night for Tommy. In a long gruelling fight between these two one would probably have to favour McCallum. It is just about plausible though that Tommy could stop Mike early. McCallum was wobbled early on by both Julian Jackson and Donald Curry. If Hearns was to land a perfect right-hand then anyone, even McCallum, would be in big trouble. Tommy also had a good left-hook and this was the punch that Jackson wobbled McCallum with in the first round of their title bout at 154.

Hearns had the speed and footwork to outbox McCallum though and if he fought an ultra cautious and disciplined fight using his legs then it seems likely that he could have outpointed McCallum over twelve rounds. Hearns, at his very best, had the speed and movement necessary to frustrate McCallum. It would certainly not have been easy though and McCallum would have stalked him for every step of the way and made life difficult.

McCallum, like Hearns, had a good jab so it isn't as if it would have been one way traffic. This is a fight in which Hearns would have had to ride out a few rocky moments and it seems more than likely that Mike would have targeted his body too. It was body punches by Ray Leonard which helped to weaken Hearns down the stretch in their 1981 superfight. My own personal instinct with this fight is that Hearns, on his best night, would have outpointed McCallum but it certainly isn't a fight I would have wanted to wager too much of my money on.

OSCAR DE LA HOYA
V
KOSTYA TSZYU

Oscar De La Hoya won several world championships in different weight divisions and took over from a fading Mike Tyson to be boxing's most lucrative star for a good few years. In fact, De La Hoya was probably the biggest non-heavyweight attraction the sport has ever produced and engaged in some of the biggest fights of all time against the likes of Floyd Mayweather and Felix Trinidad.

De La Hoya first became famous in the United States when he fought his way to Olympic Gold in 1992, determined to win for his late mother (who had recently died from cancer) and earning his 'Golden Boy' tag in the process. He was spectacular when he turned professional and, looking more like a film star than a boxer, was soon raking in the money. De La Hoya was articulate and an advertising man's dream, his bouts attracting a regular group of screaming teenage girls as if he was a pop star and his mug soon adorning billboards and magazines.

But De La Hoya, who was born in the United States to a Mexican family, always struggled to get the respect of the Hispanic fight fan community with his polished image ('a Latino Lancelot dressed in Italian suits and $400 shoes' according to a biographer) and, even worse, love of golf! They preferred more down to earth, unpretentious and stoic heroes like the great Julio Cesar Chavez, a boxer who De La Hoya would eventually meet in the ring in a time honoured youth vs experience clash.

Because he was born in America, De La Hoya was never seen as a true son of the old country like a Chavez or Marco Antonio Barrera and he alienated them further with some safety first tactics in big fights. Although he had some exciting wins and spectacular knockouts, De La Hoya always seemed more aware and concerned than most Hispanic pugilists about the fact that the person he was sharing the ring with could potentially hit him back! Mexican boxers (to a certain number of fans anyway) were supposed to be fearless sluggers not shaving-gel models who released music albums as De La Hoya did.

De La Hoya was sort of like boxing's version of Tiger Woods for a while. Obviously I'm talking about Woods before anyone realised he was sleeping with more people than Mick Jagger and James Bond put together behind his wife's back! De La Hoya grew up in poverty in East Los Angeles but soon discovered boxing - where it was apparent even at a young age that he could punch incredibly hard and had a real future in the sport if he wanted it.

Despite his polished image, De La Hoya was a tough cookie in the ring and had a wicked left-hook which he could throw from a varity of angles. He was tall with long arms and could box as well as punch. He was probably at his best at around 140 although he eventually fought for the middleweight championship before he retired. De La Hoya's victims included Rafael Ruelas, Fernando Vargas, Ike Quartey, Pernell Whitaker, Ricardo Mayorga, and Miguel Ángel González.

He was rather unlucky too in that his losses in the second Shane Mosley fight (where Mosely was later found to be on performance enhancing drugs), his superfight with Felix Trinidad, and his loss to Floyd Mayweather Jr. were all close contests that could conceivably have gone in his favour. To be fair though, De La Hoya, in the eyes of some, was lucky to get the nod in close fights with Whitaker, Ike Quartey, and Felix Sturm.

De La Hoya won 11 world titles in six weight classes, including the lineal championship in three weight classes. At his very best he was a nightmare to fight simply because he punched so hard and could back this up with good technical skills and a great jab. De La Hoya was a great fighter and for many years the money machine in boxing.

Kostya Tszyu was born in Russia but fought out of Australia. He held multiple light-welterweight world championships, including the undisputed and lineal titles between 2001 and 2005. Tszyu was a tough hombre indeed. He was incredibly strong and could punch holes in a brick wall. His right cross was one of the most feared punches of his boxing era. Tszyu made four defences of the IBF light-welterweight title and a fight between him and De La Hoya was actually on the cards in 1997. However, the fight was nixed by Tszyu's NC fight with Leonardo Mas and a surprising loss to Vince Phillips. The loss to Phillips was a blessing in disguise because it made Tszyu a much better fighter.

Tszyu rebounded by winning the WBC title and thereafter proving to be all but unbeatable at 140 pounds. He also unified the titles. Tszyu beat the talented Sharmba Mitchell twice and - in the highlight of his career - became the first person to beat Zab Judah in their unification clash. Judah was being hyped as the next superstar of boxing and was favoured to beat Tszyu but, after being outboxed in the first round, Tszyu began to get his timing and sense of distance and dropped Judah with a long crunching right hand.

Judah fell over three times from the effect of this single punch before the fight was stopped (Judah would preposterously protest that it was a premature stoppage but it definitely WASN'T - he could have been seriously hurt if the fight had gone on). Age caught up with Kostya Tszyu in the end when lost his title to Ricky Hatton but Tszyu could by this stage already be secure of his place in history. He is generally regarded to have been one of the five greatest 140 pounders in the history of the division.

Our dream fight between De La Hoya and Tszyu obviously takes place at 140 and assumes that both men are at their best and on top form. A first casual glance at this fight would make De La Hoya a big favourite given his advantage in speed and height and reach. De La Hoya would be expected to have success boxing at long range and his jab would clearly be a salient factor in the fight. The odds are that De La Hoya would be snapping out jabs and use his feet well enough to take the early rounds.

De La Hoya would be wary of a gung ho approach in this fight because he would be well aware that Tszyu would only need one punch to turn the fight on its head. Tszyu was crafty enough to time a perfect right hand on the speedster Zab Judah so Oscar would have to exercise a degree of caution. Oscar would have to make sure he kept his guard up and didn't move back with his hands down. To do that was suicide against Tszyu.

Both of these men had decent chins but they were not invulnerable. De La Hoya was knocked down several times and Tszyu was stopped by Vince Phillips. If De La Hoya got Tszyu hurt and really opened up then it is possible he could win by stoppage - though this would be unexpected. Oscar could bang but one would expect him to focus more on boxing from a distance in this fight. Tszyu's reputation as a puncher would keep De La Hoya honest. In this fight Oscar has speed and reach advantages so it wouldn't be in his best interests to get involved in a brawl with such a heavy puncher as Kostya.

Tszyu was very strong at 140. He would be capable of roughing up Oscar if De La Hoya stood his ground and got into a brawl. The key to this fight is whether or not Tszyu can land enough punches to mitigate De La Hoya's movement and win him some rounds. Tszyu is only going to win this fight if he can consistently land punches and hurt De La Hoya - which will make the second half of the fight tough and difficult for Oscar (as De La Hoya tended not to have unlimited stamina).

If Oscar gets on his bike, as he did with Trinidad, then Tszyu will be the moral victor in these rounds as far as the judges go because aggression and coming forward is nearly always rewarded in Amercan based fights. You could argue that this shouldn't be the case (most people think Oscar beat Felix Trinidad and was robbed) but it usually IS the case.

The smart money in this fight would be on De La Hoya using his speed and jab to gain a fairly clear points decision. Both men are dangerous punchers but it would obviously be in Oscar's interests to make this fight a tactical chess match given his reach advantage and more fluid boxing skills.

Not to say that Tszyu is going to sit back and happily allow this to happen. Tszyu will, in his usual fashion, patiently stalk De La Hoya and wait for an opening to throw that mighty right hand. Timing beats speed and this will be what Tszyu is banking on. The intrigue in this fight will be watching to see if Tszyu can land anything of significance. If he does it becomes a tough fight for Oscar and one that Tszyu can win. De la Hoya though would definitely start as a big favourite.

LENNOX LEWIS
V
RIDDICK BOWE

Lennox Lewis was born in London but spent part of his early life in Canada - whom he fought for in the Olympics, winning a Gold medal at the 1988 games by defeating Riddick Bowe. He returned to the country of his birth when he turned professional and fought with the Union Flag on his trunks thereafter. Lewis quickly established himself as a tremendous prospect and confirmed his pedigree when he dismantled the world rated unbeaten British champion Gary Mason in 1991.

On Halloween night in 1992, Lewis blitzed Tyson's old nemesis Razor Ruddock in two rounds and showed his vast potential. It was an eliminator for the WBC title but the holder Riddick Bowe's team clearly wanted no part of fighting his amateur nemesis and dumped his belt in a trash can, allowing Lewis to pick up the vacant belt.

After three defences, Lewis was shockingly stopped by Oliver McCall - Mike Tyson's former sparring partner - and lost his WBC title in 1994. It began a frustrating period in the wilderness for Lewis and he would have to wait three years before he fought for a title again, punching his way back into the VIP section of the division with wins over Ray Mercer and Tommy Morrison. In 1997, Lewis regained the WBC title when Oliver McCall had a meltdown in the ring during their rematch and stopped fighting. Lewis, now under the guidance of the great Emanuel Steward, finally began to fufill his great potential.

It was Steward who made the technical modifications to Lewis that brought him so much success in the latter phase of his boxing life. Steward said the incredible thing about Lewis was that despite being 250 pounds and 6'5 he was still an athlete. It was rare for someone so huge and powerful to be co-ordinated and skillful. Lewis was famous for his love of chess and often pictured over the chessboard in his training camps but this used to irritate Steward. He felt Lewis was like a chess player in the ring far too often and always felt the boxer should eschew his more analytical safety first instincts and be more ruthless.

Lewis was a pretty classy champion and cut a striking figure with his suits and dreadlocks. He was never in any trouble outside the ring, well spoken, reserved, and private. Maybe this was part of the reason why he never seemed to get the credit he deserved from the American press. They thought Lewis was dull. Lewis made four defences (including a first round blitz of Andrew Golota) before his megabucks unification showdown with the aging but still dangerous Evander Holyfield.

Holyfield had of course battered the myth of Mike Tyson into submission twice and was favoured by the pundits. However, despite a ludicrous draw verdict in their first fight (a bout that Lewis clearly won), Lewis was given the nod in the rematch (which ironically was much closer than the first fight) and finally stood atop the division at long last.

Lewis seemed to have his golden years in his thirties and with the kinks in his style ironed out by Steward he was formidable indeed with his strong jab, height, reach, natural talent, incredible physical strength, and powerful right-hand. The overhyped American prospect Michael Grant was demolished by Lewis in two rounds and the vaunted puncher David Tua barely landed a glove on him in their 2000 bout.

But a sloppy Lewis didn't bother to train or travel early to acclimatise in a defence against Hasim Rahman in Johannesburg (he'd been too busy shooting a boxing sequence for the George Clooney film Ocean's Eleven in Las Vegas) and was stopped in the fifth round. Lewis regained his world title with a spectacular fourth round knockout of Hasim Rahman in their rematch, in the process salvaging both his superfight with Mike Tyson and any status as a future great.

Lewis v Tyson was projected to be the biggest fight in boxing history. The fight was supposed to take place in Las Vegas but the Nevada State Athletic Commission voted 4-1 to deny Tyson a licence and it was Memphis that coughed up the big site fee to get the fight. Both men were to be paid a guaranteed $17.5 million. It was the highest-grossing event in pay-per-view history, generating $106.9 million from 1.95 million buys in the United States.

Tyson's increasingly unstable and erratic behaviour was of course, distasteful as it was, a big part of the appeal. Strange as it seems in hindsight, Lewis was only a 2-1 favourite and many liked the chances of a Tyson victory. Tyson had looked good savaging Lou Savarese and Andrew Golota but in his last fight a payday against the ordinary Brian Nielsen, Tyson was awful, appearing grossly out of shape and slow.

The Tyson v Lewis fight was an anti-climax for anyone not supporting Lennox and played out across eight increasingly one-sided rounds as Tyson took a horrendous pounding from the composed and much larger champion. Lewis hung around in the vague hope of a Tyson rematch and ended up fighting one more time a year later when, clearly out of shape and finally looking his age, he had a rough time with Vitali Klitschko before the Ukrainian was stopped on cuts after six rounds.

Lewis retired with a 41-2-1 record. He avenged his only two defeats, deserved a win rather than the draw on his slate, and never ducked an opponent. It is fair to say that at his best, with his great strength, size and composure, Lewis would have been a handful for any heavyweight in history.

Riddick Bowe was born in Brownsville like Mike Tyson. A tough area that produced tough fighters. Bowe lost to Lennox Lewis in the Olympics and so didn't turn professional with the world at his feet but it was clear that a mighty talent had arrived if someone could get the best out of him. Bowe was 6'5 but he had quick hands, an excellent jab, could fight on the inside with great skill (unusual for such a big man), and had good stamina and a great fighting heart. At his very best he was a formidable proposition but Riddick never quite fufilled the apparently unlimited potential he seemed to possess.

Despite his undoubted talent and raw power, Bowe sometimes seemed desperately unmotivated and was prone to putting on a lot of weight between fights. These weight fluctuations seemed to gradually sap his reflexes. By his late twenties, an age when he should have been in his prime, Bowe was already starting to look like a tired old fighter who had seen better days. Heavyweights tend to mature late but Bowe was at his best as a young fighter.

Bowe was managed by the shrewd (and sometimes controversial) Rock Newman and with the wise veteran trainer Eddie Futch to mentor him, he soon began to attract attention as a potential future heavyweight champion. He could box and punch and looked impressive blasting out names like Bert Cooper and Bruce Seldon as he climbed the rankings. A very close ten round points win over the veteran Tony Tubbs (which some felt Tubbs might have deserved) proved that Bowe was not the finished article but by 1992 he was ready to challenge Evander Holyfield for the world heavyweight championship.

In a brutal fight, Bowe proved too strong for the smaller man and won a twelve round points decision, knocking Holyfield down in the eleventh round. Holyfield threw everything he had at Bowe but Riddick showed that his fighting spirit was resolute. It was a great performance, the best of his career. The only problem for Bowe and Rock Newman was that they seemed absolutely terrified of Lennox Lewis despite a Bowe v Lewis fight appearing to be a natural.

Lewis had stopped Bowe in the Olympics and was the one heavyweight who could match Bowe's size and power. As we noted, when he won the belts from Holyfield, Bowe dumped the WBC portion in a trash can rather than meet number one contender Lewis. After winning the title against Holyfield, Bowe made a couple of shamefully safe and predictably one-sided defences against veterans Jesse Ferguson and Michael Dokes and then lost the Holyfield rematch. Holyfield fought with incredible intensity in the rematch and also used more movement. It was another tough encounter but Holyfield managed to outwork the bigger man this time and Riddick was suddenly an ex-champion.

Bowe was now in a strange sort of limbo, making do with contests against the likes of Larry Donald, Herbie Hide (from whom he extracted the lightly regarded WBO bauble) and the crude Jorge Luis González while he headed towards an inevitable third fight with the now beltless Holyfield and waited to see what would happen with Tyson's comeback. In 1995 he fought a non-title rubber match with Holyfield and climbed off the canvas to stop his old foe in the eighth round. Holyfield seemed strangely sluggish in the fight but, lest we forget, would soon resurrect his career with his infamous Mike Tyson encounters.

Despite the win, 1996 turned out to be the year when Riddick Bowe was eliminated from the heavyweight sweepstakes. In July, Bowe took a fearful pounding from Polish contender Andrew Golota and only won on a disqualification when Golota, despite being ahead on points, had a brainstorm and threw yet more low-blows (he'd been throwing them all night). The exact same thing happened in the rematch - except this time Bowe took even more punishment. When he worryingly slurred his words after the fight it was obvious that Big Daddy was finished at the top echelons of the division and should retire.

A grossly overweight Bowe made a couple of rather sad comebacks against nondescript opposition but nothing ever came of them and outside the ring he had more than his fair share of problems. A stint in the Marines lasted a matter of days and a bizarre incident saw him kidnap his estranged wife and their children. Despite the millions he earned in the ring Bowe ended up broke in retirement. It was a sadly familiar story in boxing.

Bowe's career was certainly not a failure but in retrospect it does seem a slightly disappointing one given his great natural talent. Ultimately, he was greatly eclipsed by his rival Lennox Lewis - something which must have irked Bowe. It's a terrible shame that these two gifted giants never got to meet in the ring.

So, who would have won if Lewis and Bowe had fought? A salient factor in this would be the timing of the fight. The general consensus is that if they had fought later on when Lewis was more finely tuned under Manny Steward and Bowe was beginning to slip then Lewis would most likely have battered Bowe. However, if they had fought in 1993 - as they were initially supposed to do - then this would have been much more of an even money fight where one could not be confident in predicting a victor.

The 1993 version of Lewis had yet to mature fully and was still groping for a style. The younger Lewis tended to rely on his power and could be sloppy. It was Manny Steward who made the stylistic adjustments which later turned Lennox into a truly great fighter. Still, even the 1993 Lewis, not yet the finished article, was still a super talented monster of a heavyweight. Look at what he did to Razor Ruddock.

Bowe was definitely at his best around 92/93. It was really motivation and laziness more than anything that became Bowe's undoing. Once he won the title and became wealthy he seemed more interested in eating than training and would balloon up in weight between fights. After he won the title Bowe suddenly seemed to lack motivation. Money seemed to have taken away some of his fistic hunger and replaced it with a hunger for food.

The young Bowe was certainly a terrific fighter though and like Lewis he could both box and punch. A big factor in why Bowe was so effective was that he usually enjoyed a huge height and weight advantage over his opponents. Fighters like Michael Dokes and Bert Cooper were dwarfed by Bowe and simply overpowered. Bowe would not enjoy this advantage over Lewis though because Lennox was just as tall and just as big. How would Bowe cope with fighting someone who was just as tall and strong as he was? This would certainly be a new experience for him in the pro ranks.

One weakness of Riddick Bowe, and it was something which eventually shortened his career, is that he didn't have the best defence. He always took a few too many punches. He had a reliable chin in his early years - though his punch resistance seemed to fall apart in the last phase of his career. One knock against Bowe is that he avoided most of the famous heavyweights from his era and his team clearly kept him away from big punchers. Despite sharing the same era, Bowe never fought Tommy Morrison, Razor Ruddock, Ray Mercer, Mike Tyson, George Foreman, or Michael Moorer.

Not to say that Bowe couldn't have potentially beaten these men but it does tend to make you suspect that Bowe's team felt his whiskers were not of the highest quality and so preferred to put him in against pure boxers or smaller men. Lennox also had a decent chin (the punch from McCall was just one of those thunderbolts from the blue and Lewis did actually get his feet). Lewis and Bowe, two huge powerful monster heavyweights, can definitely hurt each other though.

One would anticipate something of a chess match early on as both would be wary of each other's big right hand. In terms of boxing ability they are fairly evenly matched though one would probably say that, circa 1993, Bowe was more versatile and a better inside fighter. If this fight did unexpectedly turn into a slugfest from the opening bell you'd probably give Lewis a better chance of a comprehensive early win purely based on the way he jumped on Razor Ruddock and Andrew Golota.

We never saw Bowe in the ring against someone as big and hard punching as Lewis so we don't know if he could have taken those Lewis wrecking balls. Of course, conversely, we never saw the young Lewis in the ring with anyone as big and strong as Bowe either! Bowe would certainly be capable of hurting Lewis too if he began landing some big shots.

Lewis and Bowe, around 1993, were well matched in that both were huge, powerful and talented fighters who had good speed for their size. Both had vulnerabilities too. You could make a case for either man coming out on top.

If the fight turned into a dour tactical battle one might even e tempted to favour Bowe as he had a great jab and was a patient fighter in the ring. The young Lewis could sometimes lapse in concentration but it seems unlikely this would have happened against Bowe. Lennox would have been completely alert in the ring with Bowe at all times - given the magnitude of the fight and the danger posed by his huge opponent. Lewis also genuinely disliked Bowe. He would have hated to lose to him.

My own sense with this fight is that I would favour Lewis, even the unfinished young version of Lewis, to come out on top. This is based on the perception that Lewis would enjoy a psychological advantage over Bowe for two reasons. The first is that Lewis beat Bowe in the Olympics - and knocked him down too. The second psychological factor is that it was clearly Bowe's team who didn't want this fight whereas Lennox Lewis was desperate for it.

Lewis was 100% confident that he would beat Bowe again. Bowe's team however, Rock Newman and Eddie Futch, clearly did not want Riddick to fight Lennox. They didn't fancy this fight at all. Though one can be sure that Riddick would have fought whoever he was asked to fight, the fact that his manager made him give up his WBC title rather than fight Lennox must have made him at least question why his team didn't want this fight and whether or not they felt he could actually win.

In the end, Lewis outlasted Bowe by many years and achieved far more in boxing. In the pantheon of heavyweight champions in history, Lewis ranks above Bowe. However, in that window circa 1993, a fight between them would have been a genuine 50/50 clash in which neither would have been a prohibitive favourite.

I would favour Lewis but it wouldn't have been the biggest upset ever if Bowe had beaten Lennox. It was that sort of fight. You couldn't be completely sure of predicting who would have won. This why the failure to make this fight when Lennox and Riddick first won their world titles is especially frustrating. We were robbed of what would have been one of the most intriguing and anticipated heavyweight fights of the decade.

SUGAR RAY LEONARD
V
AARON PRYOR

There will never be another Muhammad Ali in the world of boxing but Ray Charles Leonard (later to become better known as 'Sugar' Ray Leonard) probably came as close as anyone is ever likely to get. His dazzling performances in the ring and battles with Roberto Duran, Wilfred Benitez, Thomas Hearns, and Marvin Hagler are now the stuff of legend. With the exception of a couple of ill-advised later bouts when he should have been happily retired and counting his money, Leonard's career read like a film script that you couldn't make up if you tried.

Leonard was named after the singer Ray Charles and followed his brothers into a boxing gym. When he first got hit on the nose though he decided boxing wasn't for him and left for a while. You could say that this was his first retirement! Leonard didn't really have the stereotypical boxer's background. Although his family were by no means rich (his father worked several jobs to make ends meet including a night shift in a supermarket) he didn't grow up in some crime infested place in a broken home and was always very smart and articulate.

When he put the gloves back on again it soon became obvious that he was brilliant and he won Olympic Gold in 1976. Leonard had planned to not pursue a professional career and go to college instead but he soon had a young wife and young son and an absolute fortune was awaiting him if he turned professional. The US television networks had been charmed by Leonard in the Olympics and he was already famous so he would probably have been barking mad to turn his back on boxing. Leonard earned fortunes even before he won a title because he was handsome, well spoken and already known from the Olympics (it helped too of course that he was amazing in the ring). He appeared in 7-Up adverts and commentated on fights for HBO.

Leonard's manager was a lawyer named Mike Trainer and Leonard and Trainer decided they would do things on their own terms and avoid the traditional situation where a boxer was under the control of either Don King or Bob Arum and relied on them for fights. They would arrange the fights themselves and decide who they wanted to bring into the promotion on a fight by fight basis. Leonard's reputation for doing things only on his own terms, be it picking opponents, the money he was paid, demanding that his fight with Hagler be over 12 and not 15 rounds etc, created a bit of resentment in some quarters of the boxing world.

If you wanted to fight the great Sugar Ray Leonard you had to abide by Trainer's rules - the principle one being that you got less money than Sugar Ray of course. It didn't always help Leonard's popularity in the boxing community but he was he always resolutely his own man and no one was ever in a position to steal his money or rip him off. He didn't want to be like, as he said in his memoir, 'countless other blacks who have taken up the sport since the days of Jack Johnson and Joe Louis, but have been unable to make enough money to set themselves up for the rest of their lives'.

Sugar Ray Leonard was famously a master tactician in the ring. He would research his opponent to a ridiculous degree and seek to win the fight before he even got in the ring by getting inside the head of his adversary. When Leonard came out of retirement to fight the formidable middleweight champion Marvin Hagler he did so for a number of reasons. One major reason though was that he had seen Hagler look mightily unimpressive beating the much smaller but quicker Roberto Duran on points. Leonard reasoned that he was faster and cuter than Duran and says he watched tapes of that fight so many times he could predict exactly what combination Hagler would throw in any given situation. He could read him like a book by the time he got in the ring with him.

Leonard walked out to the centre of the ring just before the bell when he fought Hagler because he noticed Hagler always liked to do that. He was invading his 'psychic space' of his opponent and playing games. He even cultivated a friendship with Hagler while knowing all along that he was going to drop a bombshell and challenge him to a fight at some point. Leonard said he would actually ban people from using punchbags in the gym when he was sparring because this was an exercise to develop the mind. The great Sugar Ray would allow no background noise from lesser mortals invading his concentration!

Against the bigger, taller and harder hitting Thomas Hearns, the boxer (Leonard) became the puncher and the puncher (Hearns) became the boxer as a behind on points Sugar Ray eventually chopped Hearns down in the late rounds to win their much trumpeted 1981 superfight. Leonard was the most successful and famous boxer of the post Ali era and engaged in a number of bona fide 'superfights' on his way to winning several world titles. He was handsome, articulate and charismatic outside the ring and the ultimate fighting machine inside. Incredibly intelligent and fast but also incredibly tough and brave. Leonard was the complete package and the greatest fighter of his era.

The volatile Aaron Pryor was born in Cincinnati, Ohio and was known as The Hawk in the boxing ring. He was an absolute fireball inside the ropes who fought every minute of every round in a furious all action style. Pryor famously beat Thomas Hearns in the amateurs and as a pro was unbeatable at 140 pounds. He won the world title from the great Antonio Cervantes in 1980 and made eight defences. Two of these were stoppages of the great Alexis Argüello.

Pryor then switched to the IBF title and made one defence but by now his drug addictions had left him a shell of the fighter he used to be. He vanished for two years and then lost a comeback fight against Bobby Joe Young - a fighter that Pryor would have demolished in his prime. Pryor is rightly regarded to be one of the greatest light-welterweights in boxing history.

Pryor had pursued a bout with Leonard in the amateurs but it never happened. As a consequence of this he became obsessed with getting Leonard into the ring in the professional ranks. Pryor knew that Leonard would give him a huge payday but it wasn't just about money. Pryor thought he could actually beat the great Sugar Ray. The fight between Leonard and Pryor was supposed to happen in 1982. Pryor's team had agreed terms with Leonard's team and the fight was due to take place after Leonard completed a mandatory defence of his welterweight title against Bruce Finch.

However, much to Pryor's dismay, Leonard suffered a detached retina in the Finch fight and retired. When you adjust the purse Pryor was going to earn against Leonard for inflation in today's money, it amounted to over two million dollars. You can understand then why Pryor was devastated to see this payday vanish into thin air with Leonard's retirement. Pryor never had much luck in this regard. He was supposed to fight the popular lightweight champion Ray Mancini but Mancini lost his title to Livingstone Bramble - thus scuppering the fight and losing Pryor what would have been a hefty payday.

So who would have won had a Leonard v Pryor fight gone ahead in 1982? Well, I probably won't surprise too many people by saying that Leonard would have been a huge favourite. The fight would have to have taken place at 147 pounds given that Ray was no junior-welterweight and this clearly would have given Leonard an advantage as Pryor would have had to come up in weight. Leonard would have been bigger and stronger than Pryor and was also a harder puncher. Pryor was fast but the edge in handspeed he enjoyed over most of his opponents would not have applied here as the young Leonard was an absolute speed demon.

Pryor's best - perhaps ONLY - chance in this fight would be to do what Duran did to Leonard in their first fight and bull and crowd Sugar Ray, taking away his great speed and footwork. However, one wouldn't expect Leonard to obligingly fall into such a scenario. He learned his lesson from the first Duran fight and would use his mobility and slick boxing skills to evade Pryor's rushes and dictate the terms of the fight. Pryor could brawl with the best of them but he was a very good boxer too. Alas though for Pryor, Leonard was the consumate boxer and would be perfectly at home in a long range chess match.

This fight would be an awful lot of fun while it lasted and Pryor would give it his best go, perhaps even providing a few uncomfortable moments along the way for Leonard, but Sugar Ray has clear advantages in terms of size, speed, power, and boxing ability and as such it is hard to conjure any possible scenario in which Leonard does not win this fight. The general consensus on Leonard v Pryor is that Sugar Ray would have stopped Pryor in the mid to late rounds in what undoubtedly would have been a highly entertaining and fast paced fight. Pryor was a terrific fighter but Leonard was simply on another level.

MARVIN HAGLER
V
WILFRED BENITEZ

It took 6 years and 49 bouts before Marvin Hagler got to fight for the world middleweight championship. No wonder he always seemed to have a chip on his shoulder! These days some boxers fight for a 'world' title after a dozen bouts. Hagler was an awkward teak tough southpaw who no one wanted to fight. After toiling for years he was ripped off when his title chance finally arrived and some blind judges concluded that he drew with Vito Antuofermo.

Hagler eventually demolished Alan Minter in London to become champion. Hagler was a shaven skulled fighter known as Marvelous Marvin. Despite his fearsome image, Hagler wasn't a brawler (though he COULD brawl) or a puncher (though he COULD bang a bit) but more of a methodical boxer who patiently ground his opponents down. Hagler could switch stances too - though he was more effective as a southpaw. It is rather unusual for a fighter to be able to box orthodox or as a lefty. Hagler was just a great all round boxer and he had one of the greatest chins in middleweight history. Not even Thomas Hearns could budge Hagler with his destructive right hand.

Hagler made twelve defences of the middleweight championship - and bear in mind this was the undisputed championship not some joke fragmented alphabet title. Hagler was a counter-puncher and absolutely devastating against fighters who came forward. Aggressive fighters like Mustafa Hamsho (twice), Tony Sibson, and Juan Roldán were all chewed up by Hagler. Hagler's finest hour came when he stopped Thomas Hearns in the third round of their 1985 superfight. If Hagler had a weakness it was against pure boxers who didn't come straight at him. Roberto Duran boxed a crafty fight against Hagler in 1983 and lost a surprisingly close decision as a consequence.

From the early eighties onwards the prospect of an encounter between Hagler and Sugar Ray Leonard was the most anticipated clash in boxing history. It would pit the fearsome shaven skulled middleweight champion Hagler against the super slick welterweight champion Sugar Ray Leonard. Thunder meets lightning. When Leonard retired in 1983 with a detached retina Hagler was devastated and the fight was filed under the 'what if?' category.

However, in an extraordinary twist, Leonard announced in 1986 that he would be willing to a sensational return to the ring for a fight agaisnt Hagler. In 1987, Leonard, who had fought just once in four years, astonished the boxing world by winning a controversial split-decision over Hagler in the richest fight in boxing history. The decision is still debated and left Hagler with a sense of bitterness that remained to his dying day.

By the time Hagler fought Leonard he was 32 and strongly suspected of being even older than that. He was clearly past his best and struggled against Leonard's speed and movement - though many believe he still won. In the actual bout itself, Leonard surprised those who felt the fight would be a mismatch by bouncing to an early lead, his old speed and skills still very much intact. Although Hagler landed the harder punches it was Leonard who got a close verdict for the upset. Hagler was very bitter at the decision in the Leonard fight and never fought again. He moved to Italy where he made some movies and enjoyed life outside the ring.

Hagler is regarded to be one of the greatest middleweights in history. In his prime, circa 1982, he was a fearsome and complete fighter. The four way rivalry between Sugar Ray Leonard, Marvin Hagler, Thomas Hearns and Roberto Duran from 1979 to 1989 is generally regarded to constitute the last golden era of boxing. Hagler did more than his fair share to build that legacy.

Wilfred Benítez was the 'fifth king' when it came to boxing's golden age. He fought Leonard, Hearns, and Duran but he never fought Hagler. Benítez was a Puerto Rican born in the Bronx. He won world titles at three different weights.

He was only 17 when he won the light-welterweight championship from Antonio Cervantes. Benítez won his welterweight title against Carlos Palomino and the junior-middleweight championship against Maurice Hope. In 1979 he lost to Sugar Ray Leonard in a tough fight where he was stopped in the fifteenth round. Benítez was known as El Radar because of his incredible ability to anticipate punches. In his prime he was almost impossible to hit.

Benítez was an amazing talent. In 1982 he outpointed Roberto Duran and seemed at the height of his powers. That same year though he later lost a majority decision to Thomas Hearns. His fall from pound for pound contender to shot fighter was alarmingly rapid. In 1983, Benítez gave a desperately lazy and unmotivated performance in losing to Mustafa Hamsho. He was never a contender again. Benítez was one of those fighters who burned out at a young age. He was never the most dedicated boxer when it came to training and the years in the ring seemed to catch up with him all at once. Sadly, he suffered poor health after boxing as a result of all those years in the ring.

A fight between Hagler and Benítez seemed a strong possibility for 1982. Benítez called out Hagler after beating Duran and announced that he wanted to become the first person to win four world titles at different weights by jumping to middleweight and challenging Hagler. Oddly though, Hagler, despite his yearning for a marquee challenger and big payday, never seemed especially interested in fighting Benítez. Benítez would then lose to Hearns and decline rapidly but a Hagler v Benítez fight would have been a very big deal in 1981 or 1982.

Ironically, one of the reasons why Hagler v Benítez didn't happen is that Hagler was supposed to fight Tommy Hearns in 1982 but this fight got cancelled when Hearns was injured.

There's sometimes a lazy perception that a Hagler v Benítez would have been a mismatch. This is clearly influenced by the rapid decline of Benítez after the Hearns fight. The 1981 or 1982 version of Benítez though would have presented a very challenging puzzle for Hagler.

Benítez fought Leonard and Hearns on fairly level terms and handled Duran much easier than Hagler did. One salient factor in this fantasy fight is that Hagler was less effective against slick boxers. He was much better against come forward aggressive boxers. Stylistically, one could argue that Benítez could have been an absolute nightmare for Hagler and bogged him down in the kind of tactical chess match that Hagler didn't especially enjoy. Hagler would have found it very hard to hit Benítez and Benítez was bigger and stronger than Duran - who gave Hagler a very tricky fight in 1983.

Given the defensive expertise of Benítez, this looks like a fight sure to go the full fifteen rounds (as fights were scheduled for in those days). One can picture a scenario where Benítez is tricky enough to frustrate Hagler and perhaps even build up a close lead on the cards. Hagler's usual counter-punching style would not be as effective as normal because Benítez would sit back and wait for Hagler to initiate the exchanges. This has all the makings of a fascinating fight (and definitely one for purists) and it would be up to Hagler to force the pace and make Benítez fight.

My own perception of this fight is that Hagler, who is the stronger man, would impose himself on Benítez in the championship rounds and also be more busy overall - thus enabling him to win a fairly close decision. In many ways it could play out similar to the fight between Hagler and Duran. What a fascinating tactical duel this fight would have been. Benítez would surely have been highly motivated for this fight and - if disciplined in training camp for a change - could have given Hagler a great challenge. Perhaps the biggest shame about this fight not happening is that it robbed Wilfred of the right to truly take his place alongside the other legends of his era. Had a fight between Hagler and Benítez taken place then we would be talking today about the Five Kings rather than the Four Kings.

SALVADOR SANCHEZ
V
EUSEBIO PEDROZA

Salvador Sánchez was one of the most revered Mexican boxers of all time. He won the WBC featherweight title in 1980 with a late stoppage of Danny Lopez. Sánchez would then go on to make nine successful defences of this title before his tragic death in a car accident in 1982. Sánchez was only 23 when he died and at the time had a number of potential big fights lined up. He would most likely have gone on to become one of the most famous lighter weight boxers of the decade. Sánchez only lost one fight - a split decision to Antonio Becerra in Mexico in 1977. He was a truly brilliant fighter.

Sánchez became a legend in Mexico after his 1981 superfight with the formidable super-bantamweight champion Wilfredo Gómez. Gómez had won 32 fights in a row all by knockout and had also beaten a number of Mexican fighters. Gómez was the betting favourite going into his fight with Sánchez but, to the surprise of most, Sánchez knocked him down in the first round and Gómez barely made it to the bell. Gómez took a fearful pounding in the end and was stopped in the eigth round. Despite the traditional Mexican/Puerto Rican rivalry, Gómez took his loss in sporting fashion and later became popular in Mexico for sending flowers to Salvador's funeral and becoming friends with the Sánchez family.

Salvador's other defences included a win over the classy Juan Laporte. In his last fight he stopped a young Azumah Nelson in the fifteenth round of a classic battle. Nelson went on to become an all time great so this was - retrospectively - an impressive victory. Sánchez only won a split decision over Britain's Pat Cowdell in another defence but it could be that he underestimated his challenger - who was practically unknown outside of Europe.

Salvador Sánchez was one of the most relaxed fighters

ever to step inside the ropes. He always seemed utterly unphased by anything in the ring. He could do a bit of everything as a fighter. He could box, brawl, punch a bit, and also use his feet very well. Sánchez had a great chin too. His punches were deceptively quick and he had long arms too so his combinations came in slashing volleys from far away. Sánchez had a chopping right hand and a good left hook. He could also adapt to his opponent's style. Sánchez often kept his left hand low as if he was preparing to catch something with it. There was a method to this madness because that low left hand could be turned into any kind of punch according to the situation.

Sánchez seemed to have the ability to freeze time inside the ring. He could stay composed and adapt to situations - even in the midst of the most obstreperous moments. Sánchez was actually under pressure on the ropes from Gómez in the first round of their fight but then dropped Wilfredo with a short counter left hook which travelled almost no distance at all. It was such a sneaky and improvised punch that most people (especially poor Wilfredo!) didn't even notice it at the time.

Sánchez was very nimble on his feet and would literally glide out the way of punches. He was difficult to nail and a very smooth boxer. He could also hold his own in a slugfest and would often punch to the body. He was just a great all round fighter. At the time of his death he was chasing a fight with lightweight champion Alexis Argüello and there was also talk of a rematch with Wilfredo Gómez. There was also the small matter of a fight with rival featherweight champion Eusebio Pedroza. Sadly, none of these highly intriguing and anticipated fights would come to pass.

Posthumously, in 1991 Sánchez was inducted into the International Boxing Hall of Fame. Perhaps the greatest 'what if?' of Sánchez's career is that when he died in 1982 the future Mexican legend Julio César Chávez was 31-0 and rising fast. If Sánchez had not died then these two would almost certainly had fought each other sooner or later at 130 pounds. Salvador Sánchez versus Julio César Chávez! What a fight that would have been!

Eusebio Pedroza was born in Panama. He turned professional in 1973. He was a bantamweight for a time and lost of a couple of early fights (including a bantamweight title shot) but it was really at featherweight where Pedroza found his groove and became almost impossible to beat. He won the WBA featherweight title against Cecilio Lastra in 1978 and held it until 1985. Pedroza defended his title eighteen times. Among those he beat as champion were Rubén Olivares, Juan Laporte, and Rocky Lockridge. The only slight blemish on his record as champion was a draw with the tricky and slick American boxer Bernard Taylor in 1982. Taylor was one of those fighters who could give anyone a tough night.

Pedroza was an exceptionally tough and determined fighter. He could punch quite hard but he could also box too. Pedroza wasn't afraid to be messy and awkward too if he thought that was his best way to win. He could be quite a rough and dirty type of fighter at times. There wasn't one thing that Pedroza did amazingly well but he was just one of those fighters who could do a little bit of everything and when this was all tallied together it made him incredibly difficult to fight. Pedroza had a good jab too and could move well when he needed to.

Predroza's title reign was highly impressive. To make nearly twenty defences of a world championship is something that few fighters in history have managed to do. Pedroza eventually lost his title to Barry McGuigan in 1985, losing a fifteen round decision. By that stage, Pedroza's long career and the wear and tear of the ring had taken its toll and he was past his prime. The youth, stamina, and energy of McGuigan was a bit too much for Pedroza that night. He still though gave McGuigan a rough night and lasted the full fifteen rounds. Pedroza was very durable at featherweight and took a good punch.

Sánchez v Pedroza, for the undisputed featherweight championship, is a fight that could easily have happened in 1982 if the stars had aligned. Had Sánchez not died tragically then this fight surely would have been made in the end. It's a bout that tends to split opinion in that one could make a plausible case for either fighter coming out on top.

It is probably safe to assume that this fight would go the full fifteen rounds. Both men are very durable and crafty and neither were explosive punchers. They tended to wear people down and get a late stoppage against tiring opponents or simply just win on points.

These two fighters are similar in many ways in that both are busy and have an uncanny ability to keep throwing punches from any position - even going backwards. This fight would not only be a trifle cagey it would also be nip and tuck. The rounds would be tight and at times difficult to score. Both have quick flicking jabs and both men are also light on their feet and tend to move around a lot. Pedroza was known for a bit of roughousing and dark arts but this wouldn't especially concern Sánchez because he could adapt to any scenario in the ring. If the fight got messy and rough then Sánchez would give as good as he got.

This fight has the potential to be awkward and difficult to score with both men not entirely dissimilar in their styles. Pedroza was a bit stronger and Sánchez was slightly more relaxed and smooth but generally they match up very well - which is obviously why this fight was so fascinating and tended to divide opinion on who would have actually won. My own guess is that Sánchez was probably slightly better than Pedroza in some key facets and would have won a close decision in a long and difficult fight. This isn't a bout though in which you would wanted to stick your neck out too much and confidently predict who was going to win though.

PERNELL WHITAKER
V
TERRY NORRIS

Pernell 'Sweet Pea' Whitaker won the Olympic Gold in the lightweight division and world titles in four different weights as a professional. It would not be an overstatement to say that he was one of the greatest fighters of all time - certainly one of the greatest of the modern era. Whitaker turned professional in 1984 and such was his talent he was moved through the ranks very quickly. In his eleventh fight he beat former world champion Alfredo Layne and one fight later he outpointed the future world champion Roger Mayweather.

Whitaker had his first world title shot in 1988 when he challenged the veteran WBC champion Jose Luis Ramírez in Paris. Whitaker easily outboxed Ramirez and clearly won the fight - only to be robbed on the scorecards. Jose Luis Ramírez was a Mexican legend and a favoured son of the WBC president José Sulaimán. Sulaimán was as thick as thieves with the promoter Don King - who just happened to promote Ramirez. Whitaker's team of Lou Duva and Shelly Finkel did not mince words after the fight. They knew they'd just witnessed a corrupt robbery.

Whitaker rebounded by winning the IBF lightweight title against the tough Greg Haugen two fights later. Whitaker battered Haugen for twelve one-sided rounds. Whitaker was a very unique fighter. He had a style that you couldn't really teach. He was a southpaw with a great jab and legendary defensive skills. Whitaker could stand right in front of an opponent and constantly make them miss. While this was going on he would pepper them with hard accurate punches.

Whitaker was fast too. Jose Luis Ramírez said that Pernell was faster than Hector Camacho. Whitaker had this bizarre but effective move where he would duck down low and roll his body around to avoid punches. He had good reflexes and footwork. If you went after Whitaker it could be a frustrating experience because the chances are you would end up hitting nothing but thin air. Pernell was simply a nightmare to fight. He could make anyone look ordinary - even foolish.

Whitaker was not known as a puncher but he could definitely bang a bit. It's not as if you could just shrug off his punches and wade in. Whitaker won the WBC title in a unification fight (and rematch) with José Luis Ramírez. He was the Ring's Fighter of the Year in 1989 and made eight defences of his lightweight belts in all. Among his defences was a decision victory over the great Azumah Nelson. Whitaker made beating Nelson look easy - which is definitely not something any other opponent of Nelson could say. He then won the IBF 140 pound title before jumping straight to welterweight.

Pernell beat the excellent James McGirt to win the WBC welterweight title and them defended his title against the great unbeaten Mexican Julio César Chávez in 1993. The twelve round superfight was scored a draw but EVERYONE knew that Whitaker had won the fight. Whitaker put on a masterclass that night but Chavez got a gift draw he didn't deserve. It was the second time in his career that Pernell had been shafted by Don King and José Sulaimán.

Whitaker then beat McGirt in a rematch (Buddy begged for the rematch but still lost handily again). You'd think that a short fellow like Pernell, who was 5'6, would have reached his weight limit but he then outboxed the much bigger Julio César Vásquez to win the WBA 154 pound title. To put that win in perspective, Vásquez had made ten defences and beaten Winky Wright.

Pernell continued to defend his welterweight titles until 1997 - when he lost a disputed decision to Oscar De La Hoya. By then he was past his prime and allegedly had problems with drugs. The incredible thing about Whitaker is that his only genuine losses came at the end of his career. The loss and draw with Ramírez and Chavez were clearly wins so you could say that Whitaker never actually lost in his prime. He was sort of like the Floyd Mayweather of his era - only (sadly for Pernell) without the acclaim and fame.

Terry Norris turned professional in 1986. He had a couple of losses in his first fifteen fights so you wouldn't necessarily have predicted he would become a world champion at the time. Norris beat good fighters like Buster Drayton and Quincy Taylor to get a 154 pound WBA title shot in 1989 against the murderous punching Julian Jackson. Norris outslicked Jackson in the first round but was stopped in the second. Jackson was that sort of fighter. He could seem slow and innocuous but then suddenly detonate a nuclear warhead on your chin. Two fights later Norris won a split decision against the ordinary Jorge Vaca (who had just been destroyed at welterweight by Lloyd Honeyghan and Simon Brown).

At this stage in Terry's career no one at all would have been buying stock in him. His record was deceptive though because Norris was an amazing athlete with gret potential. He was lightning quick and threw rapid combinations. He was a vicious all action fighter and amazingly powerful at 154 pounds. in 1990, Terry got another title shot and destroyed John 'The Beast' Mugabi in one round to win the WBC title. Sure, Mugabi was past his best by then but he hadn't lost in four years at the time. After a points win against   Rene Jacquot, Norris got a lucky break when he was chosen to be the next opponent of the great Sugar Ray Leonard. The fight was set for 1991 at Madison Square Garden. Leonard was 35 and hadn't fought in two years. He was still though the betting favourite.

The Norris v Leonard turned into a complete mismatch. Terry was simply took quick for the ageing icon and knocked Leonard down twice on the way to a lopsided points decision.

Norris got some much needed exposure from the win although it was difficult to give him too much credit as Leonard was clearly weight drained, old, and almost completely shot.

Norris beat another big name who was past his best next by battering Don Curry in eight rounds. Norris would make ten defences during his first run as WBC champion. These included a blowout of the former welterweight champion Maurice Blocker.

The most notable defence was against Meldrick Taylor -

the welterweight champion. Taylor was the man who came within two seconds of beating Julio César Chávez in their 1990 140 pound superfight. Meldrick was a terrific fighter known for his blazing handspeed. The important thing about this fight is that Terry would be fighting a big name who was still young (despite a general perception at the time that Meldrick was beginning to look somewhat burned out). Norris completely overwhelmed Taylor and stopped him in the fourth round. Terry's potent mix of speed and power was chilling that night. Meldrick was famous for his fast hands so it must have very dispiriting for him in the ring when he deduced that Terry was EVEN faster than he was.

After ten defences, Terry was a fixture at the top of pound for pound lists but in 1993 he lost his title in a shocking upset to former welterweight champion Simon Brown by fourth round stoppage. Terry was knocked down by a jab in the first round and never seemed to have his legs after him thereafter. There was always a slight vulnerability to Terry despite his frightening speed and power. He didn't have the greatest chin in the world.

Norris regained the title by beating Brown on points in a rematch. this time Terry boxed smartly and stayed out of trouble. He was a versatile fighter in that he could both punch and box. There was a strange interlude though when he lost on DQ twice to Luis Santana - a fighter he was beating both times. Norris destroyed Santana in their third fight and then made six more defences - including a unification fight with IBF champion Paul Vaden.

Norris eventually lost his title to Keith Mullings in 1997. He seemed to burn out almost overnight. The years of fighting and hard sparring had taken their toll. The frustrating thing for Norris was that at the time he was in the mix for fights with welterweight superstars Oscar De La Hoya and Felix Trinidad. Those big names had come along just a few years too late for him though. By the end of his career Terry was already slurring his words and clearly showing signs of having taken a few punches too many. It's a sad but familiar story in boxing.

Norris often spoke about moving up to middleweight but he never did. A salient factor in this is that he usually weighed about 150 pounds. He could probably have fought at welterweight - at a push. Norris desperately craved a fight with Pernell Whitaker in the early 1990s and even offered to come in at a catchweight between welter and junior-middleweight. There was much chatter about this fight in 1993 but it never happened. It could be that the Duva family dynasty, having witnessed Terry at close hand in the Meldrick Taylor fight, wanted to keep Pernell well away from Terry. So, what would have happened if Pernell Whitaker had fought Terry Norris?

There seems to be a general - if not completely one-sided - consensus that Terry Norris would have been too strong for Whitaker and probably won by stoppage. Proponents of this theory argue that Terry was bigger than Pernell, punched much harder than Pernell, and (here's the key piece of evidence) was actually faster than Pernell. One can understand this point of view because all of this was true and Terry was a frightening proposition indeed in his pomp.

However, I think there are some important factors this theory tends to overlook. The most salient factor is that Pernell was a master boxer who found a way to beat any style. And consider this: Simon Brown knocked out Norris and then took him the distance in the rematch and Pernell was much better than Simon Brown. I could picture a scenario here where Pernell frustrates Terry and makes him miss a lot. Whitaker also had a great jab and was an incredibly sneaky and accurate puncher.

If Pernell can make Terry miss and counter him then we have a scenario where the fight favours Whitaker. Terry Norris was an awesome fighter but he could be hurt and he could get tired in a long fight. I think Whitaker's ability to hurt and frustrate Terry in this fight is grossly underestimated. Pernell was never intimidated by big punchers for the simple reason that he rarely got hit!

Now, of course none of this is going to be easy. Terry is fast and powerful and Pernell's 'radar' will have to be switched on at all times. Norris will pose problems that none of his other opponents could muster. There will be some rocky moments along the way and Whitaker will have to hold and use his nimble footwork to negate Norris. This is a fight that

Norris can win but I would personally go slightly against the grain and plump for Pernell Whitaker to duck, shimmy, slide, and counter his way to a decision win in a fast paced and intriguing bout which would set up a much anticipated rematch.

MIKE TYSON
V
GEORGE FOREMAN

Mike Tyson was the last boxer to transcend the sport. While the greatest modern boxers today go about in relative obscurity outside the bubble of their profession even people who have never watched a boxing match in their lives know of Mike Tyson. Tyson was notorious. He did time for a rape conviction, bit off part of Evander Holyfield's ear in a world title fight, became estranged from trainers and managers, allowed himself to be enveloped by the tentacles of Don King, was involved in street fights and assaults, made increasingly bizarre and foul mouthed outbursts on television and at press conferences. He eventually became a circus freak show. An outcast and embarrassment to the sport.

But the young teenage Tyson was regarded to be the most exciting thing to happen to boxing for many years. He looked like a cast iron certainty to become one of the greatest heavyweight champions of all time and the saviour not just of the heavyweight division but boxing itself. He was the natural heir to Muhammad Ali and Sugar Ray Leonard as the sport's flagship star and money machine but his reign was not destined to be as smooth or as durable as most had expected.

Tyson appeared suddenly on the scene and began speedily dismantling opponents in explosive fashion, landing on magazine covers before he even had a world ranking. This intimidating character wore black trunks and no socks like an old time boxer and when he demolished Trevor Berbick in 1986 (to become at 19 the youngest person to ever hold a version of the heavyweight championship) he was compared to Rocky Marciano and Jack Dempsey. Although it all went wrong in the end, boxing has probably not seen anything as compelling as the emergence of Mike Tyson since.

After he lost to Buster Douglas in 1990 (arguably the

biggest single upset in the history of boxing or even sport as a whole) Tyson, apart from a few flashes of the old savagery and power, never really seemed to get it back together again for any sustained period and gradually lost the speed and elusiveness that made him so formidable and difficult to beat. What was once so natural became more and more difficult. Then there was prison and ever more complex legal and personal problems. Drugs, depression, money. Losing and regaining and then losing again the heavyweight championship.

Tyson had missed a spot in the American Olympic team because his all action style was better suited to the professional ranks. It is generally regarded that an Olympic Gold is crucial in establishing a superstar in American boxing (Ali, Sugar Ray Leonard, Oscar De La Hoya etc) but Tyson quickly became much more more famous and marketable than Tyrell Biggs (the American boxer who had actually won heavyweight gold). In a sense Tyson bucked a trend.

He turned professional with a first round knockout of Hector Mercedes at the Plaza Convention Center, Albany, New York, on the 6th of March 1985. "Iron" Mike was trained by Kevin Rooney, a former welterweight and disciple of the D'Amato stable. Tyson was small for a heavyweight (about 5'10) but what he lacked in height he made up for in width. He radiated strength and power and had the largest and most solid looking "shock absorber" neck (19 ½ inches) imaginable.

The key to why the young Tyson was special? Speed. He had incredibly fast hands for a heavyweight and was devastating when he punched in rapid combinations. He was also hard to hit. Tyson had been taught the "peek-a-boo" high glove defence by his mentor Cus D'Amato and also used to move his head a lot more when he was younger and so rarely presented a stationary target.

Tyson looked invincible as a teenage boxing tearaway. His fights are over quickly in spectacular fashion and few boxers have ever had such presence in the ring. Tyson looks like some unstoppable primal force and is kept busy with a constant schedule of fights. Trent Singleton, Don Halpin, Ricardo Spain, John Alderson, Larry Sims, Lorenzo Canady,

Michael Johnson, Donnie Long, Robert Colay and Sterling Benjamin all become 1985 knockout victims with only Sims and Halpin lasting beyond two rounds. "The body shot, it was like a sledgehammer!" marvels a bruised Benjamin after his encounter with Tyson.

1986 would be a fateful year for Tyson and his level competition is stepped up as a title shot begins to become a distant thought for the first time. Dave Jaco is dispatched in the first and then a big white journeyman named Mike Jameson lasts into the fifth. Fringe contender Jesse Ferguson (who later upset the Olympian Ray Mercer) takes Tyson into the sixth round in a bruising encounter. It is the first experience many boxing writers have of "Tyson Mania" at first hand and they come away impressed by the raw power of the young prodigy.

After a blowout of Steve Zouski, Tyson's first major test comes when he fights James "Quick" Tillis in May. Tillis was good enough to have fought Mike Weaver for the world title in 1981 and was a stepping stone for many young prospects. He was crafty and durable and becomes the first person to extend Tyson the full ten rounds, ending his knockout streak. You could see here for the first time that it is possible to frustrate and negate Tyson's blistering offensive and that - like all big punchers - Tyson was prone to frustration if his opponent was still there after a couple of rounds. A dubious knockdown for Tyson costs Tillis a draw on two cards. Tillis showed that Tyson was human and even one-dimensional sometimes if you were dogged and clever enough.

Tyson's next fight against Mitch "Blood" Green also lasts the full ten rounds and Tyson's marketability takes a slight stumble as a consequence. Green is from Tyson's neck of the woods and an unstable and eccentric character who used to be a street gang leader in his younger days. The pair will be forever entwined when they have a street brawl in Harlem in the early hours a few years later. The later encounter outside the ring joined the mounting evidence that Tyson was unravelling fast and not mentally equipped for fame. But back to 1986 and their legitimate fight in the ring at Madison Square Garden. Green is a huge heavyweight at 6'5 and uses an octopus like grip to hold and frustrate the shorter Tyson. Green is never in any danger of winning the fight but - like Tillis - he does present a blueprint of sorts for anyone looking to survive and evade against the young dynamo.

Eager to restore Tyson's image as a destroyer after two points decisions, his handlers throw him a couple of journeymen in the form of Reggie Gross and William Hosea. Both are dispatched by Tyson in the first round and, in June, Lorenzo Boyd is stopped in the second. The following month Tyson is back in the ring for what appears on paper at least to be a sterner test but is actually a shrewd choice of opponent - Marvis Frazier. Frazier is the son of the great former heavyweight champion Joe Frazier and Joe was also his manager, trainer, and generally everything. Marvis was a decent heavyweight who was often in the top ten and capable of using his boxing skills (he was a world class amateur) to outbox bigger men but he was also small for a heavyweight and had none of his father's power or strength.

In 1983 Marvis was 10-0 with his best wins coming against the overweight James Broad and a faded Joe Bugner when he was thrown in against the formidable heavyweight champion Larry Holmes. Holmes stopped young Marvis in the first round, showing a palpable sense of distaste for his task. As Holmes battered the groggy Frazier on the ropes after the first knockdown one can clearly see Larry compassionately motioning for the referee to stop the fight.

Although Marvis had since repaired his career to a modest degree with several wins and some decent scalps in James "Bonecrusher" Smith and Quick Tillis, Tyson's management were certain that the younger Frazier lacked the physical strength or firepower to keep Tyson at bay. The press shared that analysis and criticised Joe for making the fight in the first place. In what was arguably the most ferocious and devastating performance of Tyson's entire career, Marvis was stopped in 30 seconds of the first round, an uppercut leaving him helpless on the ropes where he slumped to the canvas. He never stood a chance of beating Tyson and Joe Frazier was lambasted for effectively sending his son out to be executed.

Tyson's world title shot was arranged for November at

the Hilton Hotel in Las Vegas. If he won he would be at 19 the youngest boxer to win a portion of the heavyweight championship. The opponent would be the Canadian based Jamaican WBC champion Trevor Berbick. Berbick was no mug and had upset the highly touted Pinklon Thomas to win the title. Although Berbick had lost three times to Bernardo Mercado, S.T Gordon and Renaldo Snipes, he was good enough on his day to have outpointed hot prospect Greg Page and gone the distance with Larry Holmes. Berbick is a strong, roughhouse if somewhat crude heavyweight and was expected by many to give Tyson a test. We can discount Berbick's points win over Muhammad Ali in 1981. Ali was a shadow of his former self and had no business being in a boxing ring at that stage in his life. Those involved in making that fight should be forever ashamed.

Berbick was slain by the forces of his own bravado and Tyson's blistering speed and ferocious power. He tried to maul and hold his ground and paid the price. After a rocky first round, the West Indian was demolished in the second, the finishing touch coming from a delayed reaction to a clubbing inside punch from Tyson as they wrested close. The punch shattered Berbick's sense of balance and took his legs away. It's still an extraordinary sight to see Berbick fall no less than three times from one punch.

Tyson fought Bonecrusher Smith next in a fight which failed to live up to expectations. In the space of twelve tedious rounds, Smith went from Bonecrusher to "Bonehugger" as he wrapped the shorter Tyson in frequent embraces and held incessantly. Smith simply went into survival mode, content to last the distance losing every round rather than try and win the fight. It was a frustrating night for Tyson and television audiences as the expected fireworks failed to appear - save perhaps for a moment in the last round when a right hand by Smith seemed to jolt Tyson for a moment. It was too little too late with Smith losing by scores of 106-120, 107-119, and 107-119 on the judges' cards. Tyson's manager Jimmy Jacobs took his own revenge on the lacklustre nature of the fight by banning Smith from appearing on Tyson undercards in the future.

Tyson's next victim was Pinklon Thomas. Thomas has a great jab and Angelo Dundee in his corner but Dundee goes 0-2 against Iron Mike when Thomas is stopped in the sixth by a blizzard of punches that could have felled a ten storey building. After a shaky first round Thomas had been doing fairly well negating Tyson's offensive thunder but once he got caught the end was inevitable. Tyson's last engagement of 1987 was a bout with 1984 Olympic super heavyweight champion Tyrell Biggs. When the pair were amateurs it was speculated that Biggs and Tyson could be the Ali and Frazier of the eighties and nineties and forge a classic rivalry. While Tyson had been sensational as a pro and looked like an all time great in the making the same could not be said of Tyrell. Biggs had squandered his natural talent with drug problems and his professional career was unimpressive so far.

The fight took place in Atlantic City and Biggs - in white trunks - used his height and boxing ability to take the first round. It was a fleeting reminder of how good Biggs might have been had drugs not wrecked his potential. Tyson soon took control and in what was regarded by many to be his greatest ever performance he battered the increasingly bloodied and helpless Biggs until the fight was ended in the seventh round. Tyson endeared himself to no one when he later boasted that he could have ended it much earlier had he wanted to and that Biggs "cried like a woman" whenever he was hit to the body. "He didn't have no respect as a professional fighter should, no class. I was going to make him pay with his health for everything he said... I wanted to do it very slowly. I wanted him to remember this for a long time."

Tyson was given a few months off and then began 1988 with a fight against the great former champion Larry Holmes in Atlantic City. Holmes was 38 now and had been out of the ring for a couple of years. The thought of him taking on a devastating young slugger like Tyson made people think of Rocky Marciano having to batter a shot Joe Louis into submission.

The night of the fight Holmes looked strangely skittish and apprehensive as he limited himself to stretching out a long left paw, trying to keep Tyson at arm's length and tie up the shorter man. It worked to a degree but Holmes barely resembled the man who had once dominated the division. He appeared heavy around the midsection and his once potent left-jab was a shadow of its former self.

In the fourth Holmes got up on his toes and started flicking jabs as the crowd began to chant his name. A patient Tyson waited for an opening and then nailed Holmes with a crunching right-hand that deposited Larry on the canvas with an audible thud. Holmes was known for his amazing recuperative powers and somehow beat the count but he wasn't going to last much longer. The former champ tried to wind up an uppercut but got his arm caught in the rope. Tyson knocked him cold with a devastating volley and the fight was over.

Holmes later said he was there for the payday and never had enough time to train. "As I neared the ring," said Holmes. "I had this weird thought: Why not be the first fighter to refuse to go into the ring? All those people watching on HBO, I'll amaze them all." Every boxer seems to have an excuse after a loss but we can maybe cut Larry some slack this time. Holmes returned to boxing again in the 1990s in his forties and upset hot prospect Ray Mercer and extended Evander Holyfield the full twelve rounds in a 1992 heavyweight title fight. The Holmes who beat Mercer in 1992 was unquestionably in much better condition and the one whacked out by Tyson in 1988.

After demolishing Tony Tubbs, Tyson then had his much hyped superfight with Michael Spinks. The fight with Spinks took place in June at the Convention Hall, Atlantic City. It was the richest fight in history and both the live gate and television audiences around the world anticipated a classic encounter between two unbeaten champions (although Spinks had been stripped of his alphabet belt he was, lest we forget, the linear champion). Tyson was a heavy betting favourite but there were plenty of experts and pundits making the case for Spinks. At the very least maybe he would play Billy Conn to Tyson's Joe Louis.

In the dressing rooms before the fight, Spinks' manager Butch Lewis, clad in a white tuxedo with no shirt, made what was obviously a big error when in his capacity as an observer he objected to a bump in Tyson's wrapping and caused a delay by insisting it be rewrapped. In the end it was Spinks' venerable trainer Eddie Futch who ended the nonsense by declaring he could see nothing wrong with the wrapping. Tyson was furious and paced around the room becoming more infuriated by the second. He told his trainer Kevin Rooney that Spinks was going to pay.

At the bell Spinks seemed to forget everything he'd ever learnt about boxing (which, needless to say, was a considerable amount). It was no secret that he was a notoriously slow starter while Tyson's record was awash with early knockouts. Spinks needed to fight the first round as if it was the fifth. He had to minimise contact and establish a jab. Was it fear that made him forget everything?

Spinks lumbered towards Tyson in clumsy fashion, initiating clinches (the last thing Futch wanted him to do because that would be a test of strength with only one winner) and throwing a few weak telegraphed right-hands that looked desperate. Tyson manuovered him towards the ropes and landed a right to the body which made Spinks take a knee to regroup. It was the first time Spinks had been down as a professional boxer. When the action resumed Tyson knocked Spinks unconscious with a right-uppercut and with only ninety seconds of the first round gone the contest was over. The Superfight had been the Superslaughter.

Tyson's life began to go into freefall at this time and he was beset with personal and business wrangles. Tyson next entered the ring to fight Frank Bruno on the 25th of February 1989, less than a fortnight after his divorce from Robin Givens. No sooner had the fight begun when Bruno took a knee after Tyson quickly rushed him with a volley of punches, staggered him inside and then sort of cuffed him down with a right that seemed to graze the top of Bruno's head. It looked as if a repeat of his wipeout of Spinks was on the cards.

But Bruno, in a brave if ultimately futile stand, started to fight back when he got up. He held Tyson with his long arms and clubbed him around the back of the head. He had a point deducted for holding but it proved if nothing else that the big Londoner would not be intimidated and had been taught how to grapple in the gym. Before the first round was over, Tyson moved in close and was caught by right-hook and then a short left-hook. His legs did a funny dance for a second and he appeared to be wobbled but Bruno couldn't land any follow up punches and the chance of a monumental upset faded.

Tyson gradually took control of the fight thereafter, his handspeed too much for the challenger. Bruno was stopped in the fifth as Tyson punished him against the ropes with a vicious assault. It had been a somewhat shambling performance by Tyson and with his personal life in meltdown one could hardly blame him for being distracted. Tyson fought once more in 1989 when he took on Carl "The Truth" Williams. Tyson seemed better able to put external distractions to one side against Williams than he had done against Bruno in January. A perfect left-hook collapsed the huge challenger early on and although he rose to his feet and told the referee he was ok the contest was terminated at 1:33 of the first round. Williams and his corner protested vehemently at the stoppage but it was hard to see the point of him carrying on. Tyson would have nailed him again sooner or later.

It was the last time anyone would see Tyson in the ring in 1989. He returned in February 1990, back at the Tokyo Dome to fight Buster Douglas. The fight was a mere warm-up for Tyson's next superfight. The brilliant former cruiserweight champion Evander Holyfield was now campaigning as a heavyweight and had established himself as the number one contender. Pundits doubted that Holyfield had the power to keep Tyson at bay but he was clearly the most credible challenge out there while a gaggle of prospects led by Riddick Bowe, Lennox Lewis and Ray Mercer were still learning their trade.

The actual fight is a surreal event, the huge Tokyo superdome deathly quiet. The polite Japanese crowd barely making a sound as the unbelievable unfolds in the ring. Buster uses his height and handspeed to box Tyson's ears off in the opening stanzas. We have seen Tyrell Biggs and Tony Tubbs start well against Tyson and then fall apart once he closes the distance and begins to unload but this time it's different. A glum looking Tyson seems disinterested and the upper body movement and combinations that made him so spectacular are noticeable by their absence. He's looking for the one big bomb but that strategy is useless against Douglas in the early rounds. Buster looks like a man reborn, snapping jabs and right-hands out, beating Tyson to the punch. It's the first time we've seen Tyson take a beating in the ring and he suddenly seems shrunken and strangely plausible. Douglas looks huge in comparison.

The Don King cronies running Tyson's corner forget the End-Swell (a device to limit bruising during a fight) and are reduced to filling a condom with water to use on instead. In the eighth round a battered Tyson seems as if he's managed to clutch victory from the jaws of defeat when he nails a complacent Douglas with a huge uppercut. But Douglas is up at the count of nine (it's obvious he was composed enough to listen to the count and give himself as much time as possible to recover) and although Tyson tries to launch a desperation attack in the ninth, Buster is soon back in charge.

In the tenth a brutal barrage by Douglas sends Tyson crashing to the canvas. The groggy soon to be ex-champion has no control of his faculties and in his woozy state tries to pick up his gumshield and shove it back in his mouth. He staggers unsteadily to his feet as the referee wraps protective arms around him and signals that the fight is over. It is perhaps the most shocking upset in sporting history.

Tyson then had blowouts against Henry Tillman and Alex Stewart before two tougher fights against Razor Ruddock. Tyson and Ruddock met at the Mirage Hotel & Casino in March, 1991. It was a bruising encounter with Ruddock hitting the canvas in the second and third rounds. He refused to fold though and gamely hung in there, even seeming to hurt Tyson in the sixth round when he managed to get off some of his own bombs. In the seventh Tyson took control and staggered Ruddock, the big Canadian reeling back against the ropes. At this point referee Richard Steele - a controversial figure already because of his disputed though humane action in waving off the Julio César Chávez v Meldrick Taylor fight with seconds to go in 1990 - stopped the contest despite Ruddock appearing to be capable of carrying on.

A riot broke out in the ring with both camps joining in the melee. There was only thing to do and that was get them back in the ring. Don King prepared the sequel for June.

The rematch was a brutal one full of low-blows, hitting after the bell and brawling violence. Ruddock hit the canvas twice and was hurt several times while Tyson had points deducted for various infractions. Ruddock ended the evening with a broken jaw and a closed eye and lost the fight on points by a wide distance. Tyson had won but the bruising encounter indicated once again that he wasn't quite the fighter that he used to be.

In July, 1991, Tyson was a guest judge at the Miss Black America pageant in Indianapolis, Indiana. There is some footage of a leering Tyson being introduced to Desiree Washington and other young women at the event. In the early hours of the morning Tyson and Desiree Washington went to the boxer's hotel room and Tyson was subsequently accused of rape - a charge he has denied to this day. In September a special grand jury indicts Tyson on rape and three other charges. Two days later, he was booked in Indianapolis and released on a $30,000 cash bond.

In February, Tyson is convicted of rape and sentenced to 10 years in prison - four suspended. The victim, Desiree Washington, was a distinguished student who couldn't be paid off or tarnished. Tyson's behaviour had caught up with him at last. His womanising, fast living, his dangerous sense of entitlement. To borrow an obvious line that did the rounds - Iron Mike had become Leg-Iron Mike. The world of boxing would spin on without him for the foreseeable future.

Upon his release from prison, Tyson had some undemanding tune up fights before challenging old rival Frank Bruno for the WBC title. Given Tyson's rusty performance against Buster Mathis Jr and the presumption that becoming a champion had probably done a lot for Bruno's confidence there were a lot more punters willing to risk a bet on Big Frank this time compared to 1989. Anyone who did have a flutter on the huge Englishman might have started to nurse doubts about the wisdom of gambling when he made his ring walk. Bruno did not look confident.

At the very least Bruno could never be accused of not giving his all in the ring. Even in his defeats, to Smith and Witherspoon, and to Tyson in 1989 and Lennox Lewis in 1993, he had fought bravely and taken the fight to his opponent when he had the chance. Perhaps Bruno was simply never given a chance this time. Tyson was, in the words of Big Frank, "on him like a harbour shark." On this night Tyson seemed to rekindle the flame of the eighties Tyson, the force of nature who seemed unstoppable. He was razor sharp and the combinations were back. Bruno could do little other than hold on desperately, trying his best to stave off the inevitable. A thirteen punch combination ended the fight in the third round and Tyson was the champion again. Well, he had one of the belts. It seemed like a mere formality now for him to aquire the others.

And so onto September the 7th, 1996 for Tyson versus the WBA champion Bruce Seldon. Bruce was on a winning streak that had seen him beat some decent opponents in Greg Page, Tony Tucker and Joe Hipp. Page and Tucker had seen younger days for sure but Seldon was getting better and many ranked him as the best pure boxer in the division. It counted for nothing in his fight with Tyson. Many Tyson opponents appeared beaten before the first bell but Seldon's surrender at 1:49 of the first round seemed especially abject. Seldon went down twice from punches that didn't even seem to connect cleanly.

Tyson seemed to be unstoppable but he was then demystified by 34 year-old Evander Holyfield. Holyfield's sluggish performance against the overmatched Czyz had everyone fearing the worst for the Real Deal. Tyson versus Holyfield looked like a shameful mismatch. The atmosphere was electric at the MGM Grand. People anticipated a short but explosive fight. Tyson came straight from his corner and began throwing right-hands as if he expected a brief evening's work. But Holyfield weathered the storm and soon began to fire back. Tyson took a moment to hitch his shorts up slightly and looked at Holyfield with a somewhat puzzled expression. The shot fighter he was supposed to massacre didn't seem to have turned up. "You the bully in there, he ain't the bully!" bellowed

Holyfield's trainer Don Turner in the corner when the bell rang to end the first.

Holyfield began to dig to Tyson's body and the champion quickly started to look confused, resorting to throwing single bombs which the experienced Holyfield was too savvy to fall for. The vaunted Tyson intimidation factor had no effect on Holyfield. As the second round ticked down, Holyfield span Tyson on the ropes and hammered some short hooks in. Tyson looked hurt. He was suddenly mortal again.

Jay Bright appears to be Tyson's chief second but he has no idea what to say to change the course of the fight. Holyfield is deliberately making it a messy, mauling inside fight and seems to be much stronger than Tyson. He walks Tyson around in the clinches and shoves him back, denying Iron Mike any leverage. In the fifth, Tyson managed to put together a flurry of punches at last, seeming to hurt Evander briefly with a barrage that was capped off with a stinging uppercut. The turning of the tide doesn't last long. Tyson is cut in the sixth and Holyfield is clearly boring in with his head. Tyson looks discouraged and is dropped hard by a left-hook. It's only the second time in his career that he's been down.

In the seventh Tyson is staggered by a headbutt but it is not ruled to be deliberate. The tenth round is a nightmare for Tyson. He's staggered by a right and saved by the bell when Holyfield follows up with an unanswered barrage. Tyson still looks groggy in the eleventh and is quickly staggered by left-hooks. Tyson reels away and the referee waves it over as Holyfield begins to hammer him again. Tyson is an ex-champion for the second time.

The inevitable rematch was set for June the 28th, 1997. Don King dubbed it The Sound and the Fury. The fight took place at the same venue. The atmosphere was even more expectant. When the bell rang Holyfield seemed to carry on from where he left off last time. He looked sharper than Tyson and radiated confidence. Once again he nullified Tyson by clinching and using his superior strength. In the second round Tyson got cut again and could clearly be seen complaining to Mills Lane about Holyfield's use of the head. Holyfield was in charge right away and Tyson looked frustrated.

Tyson came out swinging in the third. He looked mad and shoved Holyfield's head back with a forearm when they wrestled inside. Tyson, as Giachetti requested, was finally using his jab and having a much better round as a consequence. With 35 seconds of the third to go, Tyson bit Holyfield in the ear and the Real Deal turned away and began hopping around in pain. Tyson then shoved him from behind as if he was in a street fight. Everyone is now confused and isn't sure what just happened. A bewildered Mills Lane deducts two points from Tyson and the fight eventually resumes after the doctor examines Holyfield.

Now Holyfield looks mad and angry while Tyson seems to have gone crazy. They trade punches and then - astonishingly - Tyson bites Holyfield again. The extent of his second foul is only realised when the bell sounds and television replays are seen. The fight is over and chaos ensues as the ring fills up with people. Tyson is disqualified and he goes insane, trying to get at Holyfield. When Tyson and his entourage leave the ring the crowd jeers them and the boxer still seems pumped-up and out of control.

Tyson's explanation for his assault on Holyfield's tender ears is that it was retaliation for Evander's use of the head. Holyfield's tactics were rough but then the clash of heads is an occupational hazard in any boxing match. Ultimately, Tyson didn't adapt to the challenge in either fight. He didn't use his jab enough and the upper-body, head movement and rapid combinations were largely absent. Was it drugs, prison, alcohol, lack of training or age? It was all of the above and more. Tyson's life had taken its toll on the part of him that made his money as a prizefighter. Tyson won several fights after this but he was clearly no longer the fighter we remembered from the 1980s - nor even the early 1990s. Tyson's last world title fight was a dreadful battering at the hands of Lennox Lewis in 2003.

We should remember though that Tyson's prime was from 1986 to 1988. Like a lot of high energy, quick handed pressure fighters, Tyson was at his best when he was very young and could fight hard for every minute of every round. He was one of the devastating punchers in boxing history and one of the most exciting boxers ever to lace up a glove. The young Tyson was awesome and would have been a dangerous proposition for any fighter from any era.

George Foreman won the heavyweight championship in 1973 by demolishing the formidable Joe Frazier and was considered by many to be unbeatable at the time. He was outfoxed though by Muhammad Ali in the legendary 1974 Rumble in the Jungle in Africa. After he lost to Jimmy Young in 1977 Foreman had what he believed to be a mystical experience and felt Jesus had entered his soul. He left boxing and became a Baptist minister but a decade later Foreman found that his attempts to fund a 'Youth Center' in his native Houston were rapidly eating into his savings and decided to make a boxing comeback at the age of 38 to raise money for the local youngsters.

Foreman, who was known for his love of junk food, weighed nearly 300 pounds and his comeback was treated as a sad circus sideshow by the boxing press at first. However, Foreman had the last laugh when he slowly began to lose weight and ratch up win after win, eventually capturing the world title in 1994.

Foreman grew up in Houston and says he was a bit of a bad apple and destined for trouble. He credits the Job Corps with saving him and putting him back on the straight and narrow. He won an Olympic Gold in 1968 and his enthusiasm and innocence were somewhat out of kilter with others at the games. While other black Americans gave a 'black power salute' at the podium to express their anger at the political situation in the United States, Foreman was excitedly waving a small Stars and Stripes. He admits he wasn't clued up as much on civil rights as he should have been.

Foreman was a huge heavyweight with a massive 6'4 frame. He was slow but had a ramrod jab, chilling power and was adept at cutting off the ring and closing the distance between himself and his opponent. Foreman's early career was awash with quick wins and he served notice that he was a name to keep an eye on when he stopped the sturdy George Chuvalo in three rounds. In 1973 Foreman challenged Joe Frazier for the world championship. Despite his power and promise, Foreman was an underdog against the famed and formidable Frazier and admitted his knees were knocking when he entered the ring that night.

In a remarkable display of brute strength, Foreman demolished Frazier in two rounds, sending Joe to the canvas several times. Challengers Jose Roman and Ken Norton were dispatched with similar ease and Foreman was now seen as a new, more monstrous version of Sonny Liston. How ironic then that it was Muhammad Ali who showed that Foreman was beatable. Ali was a huge underdog for their 1974 fight in Zaire to the point where many feared that Ali might get seriously hurt. Ali deployed his 'rope-a-dope' and allowed Foreman to punch himself out before stopping an exhausted Geoge in the eighth.

Foreman returned with several wins while he awaited another title shot but his initial ring career had a strange and somewhat premature end after losing a fight to Jimmy Young in 1977. Foreman swapped his boxing gloves for the pulpit after experiencing what he says was a deeply religious experience in the dressing room after the fight. Foreman says he felt an energy running through him and saw the light. He says he must have appeared hysterical but feels it was a genuine experience. His trainer at the time, Gil Clancy, always maintained that Foreman was simply suffering from heat prostration and that he'd seen this happen to other boxers (right down to the particular colour of the vomit produced).

Foreman had been out of the ring for ten years when he returned in 1987 and was 38 years old (although whispers in boxing said George was older than he claimed). He was not far off 300 pounds and swapped his diet of hamburgers and pizzas for chicken and fish to shed weight. Foreman soon became something of a cult figure with his ancient trainer Archie Moore and habit of standing between rounds with his foot on the stool surveying the crowd.

He was more relaxed in the ring during his comeback and had retained the bone jarring power of his youth because one thing that boxers never lose is their punch. Foreman says that he was not just fighting to raise money but striking a blow for older people everywhere and proving that nothing is impossible. He fought in a lot of 'tank towns' and was criticised for the careful selection of his opponents but his demolition of the comebacking 'White Hope' Gerry Cooney got him a fight with the world champion Evander Holyfield. Holyfield was 28 and at his peak but the 42 year old Foreman confounded both Holyfield and the sceptics by going 12 tough rounds and losing on points.

Foreman won several more fights but a points loss to Tommy Morrison and two dreadfully tough encounters with the Alex Stewart and Axel Schulz suggested it might be time for the big fellow to finally give up the day job. However, in 1994, at the age of 45, Foreman stopped the young undefeated Michael Moorer in the 10th round to become the IBF & WBA world heavyweight champion. Quite a feat! In his last ever fight, Foreman was robbed in losing a controversial decision to Shannon Briggs. Foreman was 48 at the time.

At the age of 50 Foreman was set to fight Larry Holmes (who was also 50) in a clash of former heavyweight champions but, thankfully, the bout was canceled due to poor ticket sales. In 2004, at the age of 55, Foreman began training for a one-off comeback fight which he wanted to do to once again prove that age was just a number. This time it was Foreman's wife who put an end to this foolishness and told him enough was enough.

Life after boxing took in Foreman's unlikely new career in the world of grills. Russell Hobbs Inc had devised a new fat-reducing grill and were looking for a celebrity to become the spokesperson for their product. The age defying burger munching Foreman ('It's so good I put my name on it!') was perfect and the George Foreman Grill was born. The once surly and intimidating Foreman was now the jovial and amusing elder statesman of boxing and life in general. Believe it or not, George even got a short lived sitcom.

A Tyson v Foreman fight may have once seemed like a bizarre proposition only viewable for time travellers but it didn't seem so crazy a notion by 1990. Tyson needed to get back in the ring sooner rather than later and he was placed on a June 1990 double-header in Las Vegas with Big George. Tyson would meet his old amateur rival Henry Tillman while

Foreman would meet the Brazilian fringe contender Adilson Rodrigues. If they both won then a Tyson v Foreman fight was a strong possibility.

They both did win - both by early knockout. However, the fight didn't happen. Tyson fought Ruddock instead and then went to prison. George, meanwhile, targeted Evander Holyfield. It could be that because Tyson was a Don King fighter and George was promoted by Bob Arum that boxing politics nixed the fight. So what would have happened if Tyson and Foreman met late in 1990?

Thoughts at the time turned to Foreman's destruction of the Tyson-esque Joe Frazier back in the day. What if he nailed an oncoming Tyson wih one of those uppercuts? George seemed to have retained the bonejarring power of his youth (as the axiom goes, the last thing a boxer loses is his punch). There were even (unverified) whispers in boxing that Tyson was scared of Foreman and didn't want to fight him! Bob Arum, who promoted Foreman, was confident of a Foreman victory. Angelo Dundee also said he quite fancied Big George in this fight. He felt Tyson might be too small to beat Foreman.

The 1990 version of Tyson was not quite prime Tyson but he was still pretty good and superior to the post-prison Tyson. Tyson's main problem in the mid-nineties after he got out of prison was that he didn't have the same stamina he enjoyed as a rising fighter in the 1980s. The 1980s version of Tyson could fight twelve hard rounds with no trouble but the post 95 version of Tyson could only fight hard for three or four rounds before he slowed down. We can presume then that stamina would not be a huge problem for the 1990 Tyson.

Tyson seemed to lose his head movement after he left Kevin Rooney. He became easier to hit and less elusive. The rapid fire combinations were also less forthcoming. Too often post-Douglas, Tyson would load up on one shot rather than let fly with those devastating combinations. Still, the 1990 version of Tyson remained an awesome puncher and was far from finished. The 'second' iteration of George Foreman had better stamina than the original version. He was less explosive but much more relaxed in the ring. He could still be devastating though. The flurry of punches which accounted for Gerry

Cooney were absolutely terrifying.

Old George also had this frightening punch where he would sweep a wide hook into the side of an opponent's body. You could see the fight visibly evaporate from opponents when George landed one of these demoralising punches. George was not exactly difficult to hit during his comeback but he had a fantastic chin. The most amazing thing about Foreman's comeback is that he fought the likes of Tommy Morrison, Shannon Briggs, Michael Moorer, Evander Holyfield, Alex Stewart, and Gerry Cooney yet was never knocked down once. Big George was almost impossible to discourage. He would just plod after his opponents from the opening bell and always take charge of the centre of the ring.

Though there is sometimes an assumption that this fight would end early given that both men are big punchers it might not have necessarily turned out like that. Make no mistake, the faster Tyson would have hit George a lot had this fight happened. I suspect George would have taken a lot of punishment and may even have wobbled a few times. The question is whether or not George could have survived some rocky moments and taken the fight back to Tyson. All the evidence suggests he could.

Razor Ruddock went twelve rounds with Tyson in 1991 and fighters like Mitch Green, Quick Tillis, and Tony Tucker went the distance with the young prime Tyson. It seems plausible then that Foreman, who was incredibly strong and durable, could have done the same. The possibility of Tyson stopping Foreman can't be completely discounted but it would have taken a lot of combinations to do this and the post-Douglas Tyson didn't throw as many combinations as he used to.

George would have needed to get that telegraph pole jab going to have any chance in this fight. He would have to push Tyson back and start to land some of those big thudding punches. There was definitely something of the bully in Tyson in that he didn't like it when people stood up to him and threw punches back. If George could get through the first three or four rounds and begin to land some of those big thudding punches he would have been capable of making Tyson think twice about steaming in to attack. The possibility of an early stoppage for George can't be completely discounted but he was quite a slow starter and it seems unlikely that he would land enough punches to stop Tyson early.

My own theory on this fight might be a slightly surprising one - given that this is a clash of two legendary punchers - but I suspect this fight might actually have gone the distance. In such a scenario one would have to presume that Tyson would be the victor on points given that he would be busier and be able to throw more punches than George with his faster hands. It would be a tough fight but both men but I suspect the 1990 version of Tyson still had enough in the tank to outwork George and survive the big lumbering bombs which came his way. Still, the chances of either man landing a fight ending blockbuster can't be discounted - and this is what made Tyson v Foreman such an intriguing and exciting prospect back in 1990.

JAMES TONEY
V
CHRIS EUBANK

Who wouldn't have loved to have seen a fight between James Toney and Chris Eubank? It would have been worth it for the press conferences alone. What a contrast these two men would have been! James Toney was born in Ann Arbor, Michigan. He didn't have much of an amateur career and was (to put it mildly) something of a tearaway as a youngster. He turned professional in 1988. Despite his 'Lights Out' boxing sobriquet and the surly street gangster image he relished projecting (Toney was the undisputed master of trash talking and press conference mayhem), his style in the ring was relaxed, conservative, calculating and thoroughly old school.

Toney was a counter puncher with an airtight defence. He was one of the great ring technicians of the modern era. Toney was one of those fighters who just seemed perfectly at home in the ring. He never seemed to be phased by anything inside the squared circle. The only early blemish on his record was a ten round draw with the tricky Sanderline Williams. Williams was one of those tough durable gatekeepers who could give anyone a rough night.

Toney got his first title shot in 1991 against Michael Nunn for the IBF title. Nunn was considered to be one of the best pound for pound fighters in the world. Nunn was a 6'2 southpaw with fast hands and faster feet. Nunn had looked sensational beating Frank Tate for the title in 1987 and knocking out the talented Sumbu Kalambay inside one round in a unification fight. On the back of these performances, Bob Arum made an ultimately futile attempt to turn Nunn into a superstar.

Although Nunn had remained unbeaten, he had not threatened to become a star though. In fact, Nunn's stock had slipped considerably. His safety first style was a big turn off (his fights with Iran Barkley and Marlon Starling were absolute stinkers) and Nunn was one of those boxers who, for whatever reason, didn't seem to have much of a following or fanbase. Arum was especially annoyed when he put Nunn v Barkley on at the Lawlor Events Center but struggled to sell any tickets. Nunn had the talent to be a superstar but fans found his style boring and he wasn't very charismatic outside the ring.

Nunn had craved a fight with the forever comebacking Sugar Ray Leonard but Leonard was far too shrewd to fight him. Nunn was a classic high risk low reward fight for Leonard.

Nunn also failed to land a fight with (another of the 'boxing senior legends') Tommy Hearns. A win over a Leonard or Hearns would have been good exposure for Nunn and earned him a lot of money but to his great frustration these fights did not transpire.

Nunn was a was a 20-1 favourite against Toney. No one really knew who Toney was at the time. Nunn was rather condescending and arrogant to Toney in the build up. He was especially perplexed to be trash talked by an opponent he was expected to beat easily. The fight went according to the script for most of its duration with Nunn building up a points lead and outboxing Toney. This wasn't the fleet footed Nunn of old though. He was more stationary and this allowed Toney to land enough punches to slow down the taller champion. Toney stopped the champion in the eleventh round and became the first man to beat Nunn. Though he won more world titles Nunn never regained his lustre again.

It has to be said that Toney was not very impressive in his remaining middleweight fights. He won a split decision over the capable Reggie Johnson and then had a draw and a majority decision win in two high class fights against the veteran Mike McCallum. Toney appeared very lucky to retain his title with a split decision over the unheralded Dave Tiberi in 1992. Tiberi was so disgusted by the decision he never fought again.

The key to Toney's erratic performances at middleweight was something which would eventually hamper his career just at a point when he should have been in his prime. Toney was not the most disciplined fighter in the world. He loved to eat (Toney's mother actually ran a bakery - which probably didn't help his waistline!) and making 160 was a real struggle in the end.

Toney seemed more comfortable at 168 and won the IBF title by battering the tough but outclassed veteran Iran Barkley. He remained unbeaten and headed into a 1994 fight with Roy Jones Jr. This was the most anticipated clash in boxing at the time. No one had the faintest idea who was going to win - though Toney entered the ring a slight favourite. It turned out to be a dreadful night for James. Weakened by making the weight he was outclassed by Jones in nearly every round and lost widely on points. Jones was simply too fast for him. Toney then lost to Montell Griffin and entered a wilderness period where he became almost forgotten.

Toney did though have a famous third act to his career when, in a legendary performance, he beat Vassiliy Jirov to win the IBF cruiserweight title. Even at the higher weights, Toney's slickness and boxing fundamentals were usually enough to beat men who were much bigger than him. A pudgy Toney then campaigned at heavyweight and held his own against some huge opponents. He beat John Ruiz to win a world title but this was later ruled a no-contest after Toney tested positive for an anabolic steroid.

In the sad tradition of many great fighters, Toney then fought on for far too long and picked up some losses to fighters he would once have beaten easily. Toney was a great fighter at his best - one of the great ring technicians of any era. He had a great chin, a great defence, and an intuitive mastery of the basics of boxing. He was also completely fearless and happy to fight anyone.

Chris Eubank was born in London but actually began his career in the United States. When he returned home he gradually began to attract attention - thanks in part to his rather unique image. Eubank would wear monocles and jodpurs and speak as if he'd just eaten a thesaurus. He also openly admitted that he found boxing barbaric and only did it for the money - which certainly didn't endear him to all of his fellow professionals. If nothing else, Eubank was a character and this made him marketable. He always made his ring entrance to Tina Turner's Simply the Best and vaulted over the ropes. Eubank's theatrical ring entrances were clearly an influence on Prince Naseem.

Eubank could fight too. He was incredibly strong and had a cast iron chin. He could bang a bit but was more of a boxer than a puncher. He was a crafty sort of fighter with a good ring IQ and also incredibly tough and brave. Make no mistake, Eubank was not an easy night's work for anyone. In a huge domestic fight, Eubank beat Nigel Benn to win the WBO middleweight title in 1990. The WBO title was lightly regarded then (you could argue it still is - do we really need four world title belts?) but the WBO was embraced in Britain (probably because its existence made it easier for promoters to stage 'world' title belts and for ordinary British fighters to become champions) and the WBO found Britain to be a lucrative market for sanctioning fees.

Eubank's second defence of his title was a controversial points win against the tough and talented Michael Watson. A rematch was arranged (this time for the 168 pound WBO belt) and an inspired Watson was on the way to victory in the rematch until he was stopped late in the fight - which left him fighting for his life with a brain injury. Watson survived, though with life changing injuries. Eubank was greatly distressed by the events of that night and it is often speculated that he lost his killer instinct as a result. Eubank always seemed content to go the distance thereafter. Sometimes he would knock someone down and then not even go after them.

Eubank made sveral defences of his 168 pound belt though truth be told his WBO mandated opponents sometimes left something to be desired. Fights with American stars like Toney, Nunn, and Jones Jr were never made and Eubank was perfectly content to just fight in Britain against WBO challengers. Eubank seem to go off the boil in the end and was very lucky to escape with draws against Ray Close and his old nemesis Nigel Benn in a rematch. He eventually lost his title to Steve Collins - though by that point he was past his best and only fighting for the money.

In his prime Eubank was a terrific fighter and so it remains frustrating that he never ventured to the United States to fight the big names over there. Eubank's reputation though was already secure through his dramatic and ultimately tragic fights with Benn and Watson. So, who would have won if a fight between Toney and Eubank had been made? The most likely time for this to have happened would have been somewhere around 1992 or 1993 at super middleweight. It is unlikely they could have fought at 160 because they were less well known then and Toney struggled to make that weight - as too did Eubank in the end (he abandoned 160 pounds in fairly rapid fashion once he picked up a belt).

A fight between these two colourful characters would in all likelyhood have been something of a tactical chess match. Eubank liked to sit back and take a good look at his opponent and Toney was a natural counter puncher. In terms of punching power these two are fairly even in that neither were noted knockout punchers but they were both quite heavy handed. A knockout seems highly unlikely in this fight because both had cast iron chins and were as tough as old boots.

Toney took punches from heavyweights later in his career while Eubank was only stopped in his last fight against the big punching cruiserweight Carl Thompson (and that stoppage was the result of a swollen eye). Both of these fighters are also defensively sound - especially Toney. Toney was almost impossible to hit with clean punches. If we presume then that this fight probably goes the distance (which is clearly the most plausible scenario) the outcome will depend on who can win the majority the of the rounds. Who is the better pure boxer and who is likely to be busier?

Toney got a reputation for being lazy in the ring during the more fallow years of his carer after the Jones loss but when he was a champion and fully switched on he was terrific fluid boxer with sublime skills. One suspects that Toney, at his best, would be able to outbox Eubank sufficiently to edge the scorecards - especially early in the fight as Eubank could be a slow starter. Eubank tended to fight at his own pace and only go through the gears when he had to.

If Eubank was ever down in a fight with time running out he would usually go on the attack. Eubank was always dangerous in the later rounds. He would plant his feet and let the big shots go and he was a good body puncher too. These two fighters are both exceptionally tough and also intelligent enough to adjust their strategy according to their opponent. One suspects that Toney would deduce how strong and tough Eubank was and elect to use his boxing skills as his passport to victory. It would make no sense for Toney to get into a brawl with Eubank because that would not be playing to his strengths.

Toney could brawl and fight on the inside but it would risky to do that with Eubank because Eubank would be unlikely to yield and might even outlast Toney in such a fight when it came to stamina. My own view on this fight is that Toney would probably win a fairly close decision in a fight with drama and tension with no knockdowns. One can picture a scenario where a late rally by Eubank gives Toney a rough ride at times but still leaves Eubank a few rounds down on the scorecards.

WLADIMIR KLITSCHKO
V
VITALI KLITSCHKO

The huge Ukrainian heavyweight Wladimir Klitschko had his
setbacks as a professional but was intelligent enough to learn
from his mistakes and adapt his style. Fighting tall and using
his immense height, reach, jab, and power, he managed to
dominate the division with a longevity that must be respected.
Wladimir was the 1996 Super Heavyweight Gold Medalist at
the 1996 Olympics in Atlanta and although he sometimes
seemed to be in the shadow of his brother Vitali in the early
days he perhaps proved to be the more adaptable boxer in the
end.

The knock against Wladimir is that he benefited from a
weak era for the heavyweight division but - to borrow a well
worn cliche - he could only beat what was put in front of him.
Ali's legend was secured by the incredible supporting cast of
Liston, Frazier, Foreman, Norton et al. Few other heavyweight
champions though fought in such an era. One could be
pedantic and argue that Larry Holmes didn't have the greatest
roster of challengers either in his long reign. Great
heavyweights were also thin on the ground when Mike Tyson
ruled the roost.

When Joe Louis made 25 defences of the heavyweight
title his toil was often dubbed the "bum of the month club"
because of the perceived weakness of many of his challengers.
Rocky Marciano retired undefeated but he only made six
defences of the heavyweight title and didn't stick around to
fight Floyd Patterson. The point is not to discredit any of these
men, all great fighters and champions, but merely to
remember that boxers can only beat the best of their own era -
not travel in time machines!

After building up an early winning streak, Wladimir
suffered his first loss by late stoppage to journeyman Ross

Puritty. Wladimir needed to work on his stamina and seemed to improve in putting together an unbeaten run that included victories over Ray Mercer, Jameel McCline, and Chris Byrd. However, in 2003, he was stopped in two rounds by the hard-punching South African Corrie Sanders and suffered a further setback in 2004 when Lamon Brewster stopped him in five. Wladimir came up with various daft conspiracy theories to explain his loss to Brewster. It's safe to say that he didn't take that defeat in sporting fashion.

Wladimir bounced back, picking up most alphabet versions of the championship (save for the WBC belt which his brother held) along the way. He beat Brewster in a rematch, the tough Nigerian Samuel Peter, former champ Hasim Rahman, the dangerous Russian Alexander Povetkin, and the former cruiserweight champion David Haye, amongst many others.

Wladimir seemed to fight in a semi-crouch in his younger years and it was this style that seemed to prove his undoing against Sanders in particular.

It's a well worn axiom that heavyweights mature late and this was certainly the case with Wladimir. Fighting tall and using his jab like a barge pole to keep his opponent at distance, the Ukrainian has looked almost unbeatable at times in his 30s. Wladimir eventually lost his title to the British challenger Tyson Fury. Wladimir found it difficult to fight someone who, just for once, was bigger than him, and Fury's feints, boxing ability, and jab were puzzles that Wladimir never managed to solve. By that stage though Wladimir was well into the veteran phase and past his prime.

Vitali Klitschko won the lightly regarded WBO belt by walloping Herbie Hide (Hide was a talented but fragile fighter who had fast hands but a weak chin - Hide was also very small for a heavyweight and later campaigned at cruiserweight) and later made several defences of the WBC title. His only two defeats came against Chris Byrd and Lennox Lewis. Vitali was pulled out of the Byrd fight with a shoulder injury - though he was plainly tiring and struggling. He fought well against Lennox Lewis but was stopped on cuts. Lewis was overweight and somewhat past it at the time and never fought again.

As with his brother, the knock against Vitali is that he fought in a weak era for heavyweight boxing. Vitali's title defences came against the likes of Danny Williams, Chris Arreola, Kevin Johnson, and Tomasz Adamek. Not exactly a legendary gallery of challengers. Still, as with his brother, you can only beat what is front of you! It wasn't Vitali's fault that he didn't box in a more rich and challenging era for the heavyweight division. If he'd been in his prime in the early 1990s then Vitali would have found himself up against the likes of Bowe, Holyfield, (young) Lennox Lewis, Tyson, Foreman, Morrison, (prime) Mercer, Ruddock, etc. The era that Vitali fought in was very poor by comparison.

Vitali Klitschko was a terrific fighter though. He was huge, could punch hard, and had a great chin. He was quite awkward too with his long arms - which made him difficult to fight. Vitali would usually impose himself on his opponents and simply overpower them. He was an incredibly strong and powerful man. The only other heavyweight on his level during his prime was brother Wladimir. Now, these two never fought in the ring for obvious reasons. Blood is thicker than water and all that. But what would have happened if they had? Who would have come out on top in a fantasy fight between the towering Klitschko brothers?

Vitali was more durable than Wladimir and mentally stronger. One always had the impression that Wladimir was more likely to unravel in a tough fight than Vitali. There was a question over Wladimir's chin and, as we have noted, he was stopped more than once. Wladimir solved this issue later though by adopting a safety first style where he became very difficult to tag with a clean punch. He would control the distance and keep his opponent at arm's length. Given the fact that nearly all of his opponents were smaller than him

This proved to be highly effective. Wladimir's jab and clutch tactics wouldn't work against a fighter as big as him though so he'd have to modify his strategy somewhat in this fantasy fight.

The advantages Wladimir had over Vitali? Wladimir was a better and more fluid boxer and also probably punched harder than his brother. Wladimir was more textbook that

Vitali

and his punching was more crisp. Wladimir also could box to a plan and adopt a strategy whereas Vitali was a trifle more crude and would simply rely more on his size and strength to get the job done. All in all, Wladimir seemed more savvy and calculating than his brother in the ring. Vitali admitted that Wladimir was a better pure boxer than him.

Given that Wladimir had the weaker chin, should there be a knockout in this fight it seems much more likely that Vitali would be the man claiming the victory. Vitali had a fantastic chin. Vitali took punches from Lennox Lewis which would have wrecked anyone else but he still stayed on his feet and kept fighting back. Vitali was ruthless if he got a man going so Wladimir would be in big trouble if he was hurt or wobbled. Wladimir certainly has the power to make Vitali think twice about steaming in but it seems reasonable to suggest that Vitali is the less likely of this pair to hit the canvas in this fight. He simply had a much better chin than his brother. Wladimir could certainly punch but Vitali was almost impossible to hurt.

Vitali was the more aggressive fighter out of the two and it would be him that ploughed forward looking to initiate the action and get into a real fight. Wladimir would look to box more and keep the fight at distance. He'd tried to control the tempo and wait for the right openings. Both men would probably be wary of each other's power - which could make it a bit of a chess match early on. The expected fireworks may not actually transpire here. It could instead be a cagey and tactical fight.

My own guess is that Wladimir would be intelligent enough to come up with a strategy which would enable him to outbox Vitali over enough rounds to secure a clear but close points decision. He would almost certainly though have to weather some rocky and difficult moments along the way.

JACK DEMPSEY
V
HARRY WILLS

Jack Dempsey was the world heavyweight boxing champion for most of the 1920s and eventually became one of the most beloved sporting icons in American culture. There are a pantheon of heavyweight champions that are set slightly apart from the rest because they became mythic figures that seemed to encapsulate their age and (for better or for worse) made an emotional connection with the wider public beyond the boxing bubble. Jack Johnson, Muhammad Ali, Joe Louis, Jack Dempsey. Rocky Marciano perhaps.

Born in 1895 in Manassa (hence his nickname - The Manassa Mauler), Dempsey was from a poverty stricken background and worked hard labour intensive jobs when he was still a child. He rode freight trains as a hobo during the depression looking for work and competing in "toughman" contests in mining camps in Utah, Nevada and Colorado. Legend has it that Dempsey once walked thirty miles across the desert to earn $20 for a fight. He won most of them but took a few beatings too, remembering having to be carted out of one contest in wheelbarrel. It soon became apparent though that the incredibly strong and determined Dempsey had the makings of a boxer and that his true destiny was to become the heavyweight champion of the world.

Dempsey was 6'1 and not especially big (he would be a cruiserweight or light-heavyweight rather than a heavyweight if he was boxing today) but he was magnificently proportioned with powerful shoulders and arms and absolutely ferocious in the ring, swarming all over his opponents and fighting every round as if it was the last. When the young Mike Tyson first emerged in the eighties the fighter he was most compared to by boxing writers for his aggressive take no prisoners style was Jack Dempsey.

Dempsey is generally regarded to be one of the hardest punching heavyweights of all time (he would soak his hands in brine to toughen them up and when he won the title from Jess Willard his punches seemed so destructive there were rumours he had his hands encased in plaster of paris under his gloves - rumours that were completely false of course) and was involved in the first ever fight to generate a million dollar gate. He was married to a silent film star and seemed to be a living symbol of the Jazz age and America, proof that anything was possible no matter where you came from.

Dempsey had Jewish, Cherokee and Irish ancestry and writers like Ring Lardner following his every move and establishing his legend in print. He was one of the first athletes to be marketed in a fashion that resembles today's sporting world. He had endorsements, made a fortune from exhibitions and personal appearances, even had a Hollywood film contract at one point and would take part in publicity events like a photoshoot in the gym with Houdini (rather in the manner that the young Ali was once photographed clowning around with The Beatles). But despite his reputation as a great gentleman, star and popular man of the people (a real life Rocky Balboa if you will), it wasn't quite so straight forward as it appeared for Dempsey and - like Muhammad Ali - he had to work hard to gain the acceptance and love of the American public.

Dempsey's prime came in a fascinating decade in American life. There seemed more writers than ever, it was a time of hedonism and style, gangsters, Al Capone, bootleggers, endless nightlife and bright lights. Demspey was a like a metaphor for the growing wealth and power of the United States. It's surprising how inactive Dempsey was at times. He only fought a handful of defences over several years. If a boxer did that today he'd be stripped of his title but in those days boxers and their promoters were bigger than boxing organisations.

Dempsey was as much a celebrity as a boxer at times and he and his film star wife Estelle Taylor must have been rather like the American Posh Spice and David Beckham of their day one imagines. Although Dempsey was destined to become a hero the strange thing is that it only really occurred late in his career when he lost to Gene Tunney. When Dempsey was twenty years-old he married a piano player and former prostitute fifteen years his senior named Maxine Cates. When their relationship went sour, Cates claimed Dempsey had dodged the draft in World War I and he suddenly became very unpopular.

Despite his genuinely poor background, Dempsey was also (rather strangely) seen as something of a fraud by the public because much was made of the freight train riding hobo who had become champ and yet he always seemed to be the epitome of wealth and glamour with his sharp suits and chiselled features. Dempsey was tried in a Federal court and cleared of all the draft dodging charges, indeed later serving in the coast guard during World War 2.

Two fascinating characters in Dempsey's career were Doc Kearns, a shrewd hustler who Dempsey throws his lot in with when he can't get fights and moved to San Francisco, and Tex Rickard, the manager of Madison Square Garden (who staged most of Dempsey's big fights). Both were larger than life characters who could only have existed in the Jazz age. Rickard turned the arena into an entertainment centre and would keep writers and journalists sweet with free tickets and booze. As far as public relations went he was way ahead of his time.

The famous title winning effort against Jess Willard ushered in the Dempsey era. Willard was 6'6 and outweighed Demspey by over 50 pounds but he was ruthlessly chopped down in three rounds by his smaller but much more feral challenger. After all those toughman contests it made no odds to Dempsey how big his opponent was. He didn't care. In his fight with Luis Firpo, Dempsey was knocked clean out of the ring and somehow managed to get back in and win the fight. It's regarded to be a classic.

Dempsey eventually lost to Gene Tunney and past his prime. Dempsey was 31 now and a huge star. He wasn't fighting much but spending more time as a celebrity. He had been paid $1 million by Universal to appear in silent films but felt this hadn't really worked out as well as he hoped. He approached flamboyant promoter Tex Rickard to suggest an attractive opponent and the obvious choice was Gene Tunney. Tunney was a scholar who didn't even like boxing much. He quoted Shakespeare and read Troilus and Cressida and listened to opera while in training camp. He seemed dull compared to Dempsey and so Dempsey was the sentimental favourite.

Tunney was a deserving contender and like Dempsey he was white, handsome and of Irish blood. They fought in Philadelphia in 1926 before a crowd of 135,000 and the rusty Dempsey was comprehensively outboxed by Tunney. Some people were so astonished at seeing the feral Dempsey tamed in this fashion that they assumed the fight must have been fixed. A year later they fought again at Soldier Field in Chicago and the 'long count' incident is still part of boxing folklore.

Just like the first fight, the brawling Dempsey was being outboxed but he launched a ferocious attack in the seventh and knocked Tunney down for the first time in his career. The problem was, a new rule change had recently come in where boxers had to go to a neutral after they'd knocked a man down before a count could start. Dempsey had been used to standing over the poor fellow he'd just knocked down and clobbering him again as soon he tried to get up. He completely forgot about the rule change and stood impatiently next to his fallen opponent waiting for a chance to finish it.

The referee started counting and then realised Dempsey was not in a neutral corner. He started a new count when Dempsey finally went to a corner to wait and by the time Tunney unsteadily got to his feet he had been given a combined count of fourteen seconds. Would Tunney have beaten a count of ten? It's been debated ever since. Tunney spent the day of the rematch relaxing reading a copy of Somerset Maugham's Of Human Bondage. The author tells us that one of Dempsey's bodyguards grew extra confident before the first fight when he saw Tunney reading. Surely, he reasoned, someone who reads books can't possibly be capable of beating the murderous Jack Dempsey!

Tunney had the sense to get out of boxing while he was still unscathed and somewhere near the top of his game. He was too smart to ever allow himself the fate of many ex-champions, that of a name 'opponent' for young prospects to add to their record in some tank town. It helped of course that Tunney didn't have to worry about money but he never had the basic love or appetite for boxing that many great champions so obviously did.

Jack Dempsey believed defeat was the making of him though and he became more popular than ever because of the sportsmanlike fashion in which he accepted it. He could barely walk after the fight he asked for assistance just so that he could go and shake Tunney's hand. The second fight generated a gate of $2.6 million - amazing figures for the era. Dempsey lived a long life and so was able to enjoy the fame and reverence that his career inspired.

Harry Wills (born 1889) was a black heavyweight boxer from New York considered one of the greatest of his era. He was known as The Black Panther. However, he never received a shot at the world title because of the 'color bar' where white champions refused to fight black contenders. Wills came frustratingly close to securing a fight with the legendary white champion Jack Dempsey in 1926 but it never happened in the end. Wills always believed he would have won such a contest. Sadly, we'll never know who would have prevailed in a match between these two great boxers. Wills was posthumously inducted into the International Boxing Hall of Fame in 1992.

Jack Dempsey did not defend his title against black boxers in what was a very sad reflection of the times. His managers could make a fortune fighting white boxers and after the flamboyant black heavyweight champion Jack Johnson had provoked race riots and become public enemy number one in the previous decade, the boxing authorities were in no rush to have another black champion again so soon.

When he was the first black heavyweight boxing champion, Jack Johnson was brash and flamboyant. Johnson paid no attention to the segregated laws of the day and racist attitudes. He flaunted his money, had white wives and girlfriends, and mocked his white opponents in the ring. "While most black people struggled to survive," wrote one of his biographers. "He revelled in his riches and fame. And at a time when the mere suspicion that a black man had flirted with a white woman could cost him his life, he insisted on sleeping with whomever he pleased. Most whites saw him as a perpetual threat - profligate, arrogant, amoral, a dark menace, and a danger to the natural order of things."

The establishment had its revenge on Johnson when he was arrested and convicted in 1912 for violating the Mann Act, a law that banned the transportation of women in interstate or foreign commerce for the purpose of prostitution, debauchery, or for any other immoral purpose. The law was designed to stop organised prostitution but Johnson, traveling with a white woman, was reeled in under the act and forced to flee the country, later serving a year in prison. The still controversial nature of Johnson's life was indicated decades later when President Obama ignored lobbying to give Johnson a pardon (it was actually President Trump who granted the pardon in the end). The world's first black heavyweight champion, all these years later, was still too infamous for America's first black President to want to be linked to.

Wills was left to fight for so called 'colored heavyweight championship' many times. His 89 wins included 56 knockouts. He was a powerful man who could punch - especially with the right hook. Wills beat Firpo easier than Dempsey though he did lose by DQ to Jack Sharkey in 1926. The failure of a Dempsey v Wills fight to occur was apparently no fault of Dempsey. He wanted to fight Wills but said the bout never happened because they could never find a venue. Dempsey and Wills actually signed a contract to fight each other in 1925 but the bout fell through when Dempsey's fee for the fight failed to be forwarded to him. Wills twice tried to sue for breach of this contract. Despite all of this though he never got to fight Dempsey for the title.

So who would have won if these two had fought? One could argue that Wills fought better competition than Dempsey and he was also much more active. Wills was much bigger than Dempsey at 6'3 and 210 pounds although, as we know, Dempsey wasn't bothered at all by fighting bigger opponents. Perhaps the most salient factor in this fight is timing. By 1925/26, Wills was past his best. The question becomes this: would Wills have had enough left in the tank to beat Dempsey circa 1925? Many believe Wills would have beaten Dempsey had the fight taken place five years earlier. Obviously we have no way of knowing this for sure though. Dempsey was an incredible puncher capable of beating anyone he managed to hit.

Wills was adept at wrestling and rough tactics and he could bang too. He wouldn't have been phased by a rough scrappy sort of fight of the type that Dempsey would surely seek to instigate. Wills would be capable of hurting Dempsey too so it isn't as if Jack would be the only person capable of a knockout in this fight. The odds of a long grueling sort of fight are not as long as you might think. If this was the sort of fight which transpired you'd probably favour Harry as he was a better boxer and also much more active than Dempsey.

Dempsey v Willis in 1925/1926 is a fight that Wills CAN win but logic probably dictates that Dempsey, who had more left in the tank at that stage of his career than Wills, would have found a way to come out on top and stop Wills. Had the fight taken place a bit earlier then the possibility of a Wills win would be much greater though. The great tragedy of this debate is that Harry Wills never got a chance to fight for the title and answer this decades long debate over who would have won out of him and Dempsey once and for all.

EVANDER HOLYFIELD
V
MICHAEL SPINKS

Evander Holyfield won the world heavyweight championship several times but (unfortunately) is best known for having part of his ear bitten off by Mike Tyson in their infamous 1997 rematch. Holyfield was born in 1962 in Alabama as the youngest of nine children. When he was still a toddler the family moved to Atlanta. Holyfield's all action fighting style stemmed from his amateur days according to the boxer and memories of getting the short end of the stick when he fought white fighters.

A fight with Steve Kirkwood in particular seemed to leave a heavy impression on him. "I just stood there for a second, fighting to keep the pain and humiliation from my face, and then walked back to my corner to get my gloves unlaced. I didn't do anything because Stevie Kirwood was white, and one thing a black fighter in the Deep South learns early on is that knockouts -- clean knockouts -- are the only way to guarantee a victory against a white kid. Anything else is a crapshoot. So when the decision went to Stevie I did what I'd done before on those rare occasions when I'd lost a decision to someone I was sure I'd beaten: I did nothing."

Holyfield still worked as a salesman in a car dealership (hence his 'Real Deal' sobriquet) in Atlanta when he first turned professional in 1984. He wanted a stable career that he could fall back on after boxing but he ended up making such ridiculous amounts of money it wasn't necessary. Just to put it in perspective, Holyfield earned $34m alone just for his second fight with Mike Tyson. Holyfield had only won Bronze in the Los Angeles Olympics because he was disqualified after hitting the New Zealander Kevin Barry with a low blow.

Many felt Holyfield should not have been disqualified though and it cost him a certain Gold. There is a certain cache to a boxer with an Olympic Gold so Holyfield was initially in the shadow of stablemates like Mark Breland, Tyrell Biggs and Meldrick Taylor when he switched to the paid ranks with the Duva family promotional stable. Holyfield was a cruiserweight too which didn't help. The cruiserweight division was formed in the eighties and sits in between the heavyweight and light-heavyweight divisions. It was a rather unloved weight class at the time and dismissed as a place for overweight light heavyweights and small heavyweights.

Holyfield was sensational though as a professional and cleaned the division up. His most notable fight was (winning the title) against Dwight Muhammad Qawi, a snarling 5'6 boxer known as The Camden Buzzsaw. Qawi was a savvy veteran and a fierce competitor and he and Holyfield fought 15 extraordinary rounds. Holyfield got the decision but ended his night in hospital being treated for dehydration. Holyfield was a junk food junkie at the time and it was always heaven to indulge himself after a fight with milkshakes and apple pies and whatever he felt like. It was a great relief when he moved to heavyweight and didn't have to make 195 pounds anymore.

Holyfield had to add 20 pounds of muscle before dipping his toe in heavyweight waters and although always small by heavyweight standards he fought on level terms with huge monsters like Riddick Bowe and Lennox Lewis. Even when he was only a cruiserweight, shrewd judges were already marking him down as the man who might burst the Mike Tyson bubble one day because it was inevitable that he would rise to heavyweight and fight him eventually.

But by the time Holyfield was ready for a title shot, Tyson had been upset by the unfashionable James "Buster" Douglas. Douglas decided to defend against Holyfield rather than give Tyson an immediate rematch. It was a fascinating match-up on paper. Could Buster fight with the same motivation he'd displayed against Tyson? Was Holyfield big enough to compete at heavyweight? Could he negate Buster's size advantage?

The fearless predictors were split but the actual fight proved to be a dreadful anti-climax. Buster was hopelessly overweight and fought like a man thinking about what he might have for dinner that evening rather than a man defending the world heavyweight championship. When Douglas went down in the third he appeared to be perfectly capable of getting up but seemed to make a conscious decision to stay on the canvas.

Holyfield was regarded at the time to be a somewhat tainted champion and this feeling was exacerbated when Tyson was convicted for rape in 1992. Tyson and Holyfield had been scheduled to fight in 1991. Most pundits had felt that Tyson would overpower Holyfield and so Holyfield surely couldn't win whatever he did while Tyson was in prison. Sans Tyson, Holyfield beat the veterans George Foreman and Larry Holmes on points but lost his title to the talented young Olympian Riddick Bowe.

The 6'5 Bowe dwarfed Holyfield and used his raw power and infighting skills (Bowe was very adept at infighting for such a huge man) to great effect. What was arguably Holyfield's finest hour followed when he upset Bowe in the rematch, winning a hard fought decision in a superb display of speed, discipline and determination. It was our first reminder that Evander Holyfield was never a man one should be too quick to write off.

The Real Deal endured a choppy period next with lingering rumours about his health. He seemed strangely lethargic losing his title to the hot and cold Michael Moorer and stories about a heart condition suggested retirement. He was back soon enough but when he lost his (non-title) rubber match with Bowe by eighth round knockout (the first time Holyfield had been stopped) his days at the top seemed numbered. But Tyson was out of prison by 1995 and seemed back to something near his formidable best when he destroyed Bruce Seldon and Frank Bruno to pick up a couple of the alphabet titles. Don King was eager to avoid Lennox Leis and so, looking around for an attractive but beatable opponent to continue the Tyson moneymaking juggernaut, settled on Holyfield.

Tyson would have been a prohibitive favourite had they clashed in 1991 and the odds in his favour had only increased by 1996. Holyfield's last fight before tackling Tyson was a desperately underwhelming five round victory against the former light-heavyweight champion Bobby Czyz. The 5'9 Czyz, who started his professional career as a middleweight, was having his first heavyweight bout and seemed dwarfed by Evander. Holyfield's sluggish performance against the overmatched Czyz had everyone fearing the worst for the Real Deal. Tyson versus Holyfield looked like a shameful mismatch.

At the MGM Grand the now 34-year-old Holyfield astonished everyone by dismantling the lingering myth of Tyson in eleven one-sided rounds. Holyfield (who seemed so large and muscular that steroid rumours dogged him for the rest of his career) defied the oddsmakers and took charge of the fight early on, refusing to concede ground to Tyson and shoving the shorter man back with brute strength. Holyfield began to dig to Tyson's body and the champion quickly started to look confused, resorting to throwing single bombs which the experienced Holyfield was too savvy to fall for. The vaunted Tyson intimidation factor had no effect on Holyfield. Holyfield decked Tyson in the sixth with a left-hook and battered him so completely in the tenth and eleventh rounds that the referee's intervention was unavoidable. A mighty upset had occurred.

Despite his heroics, Holyfield found himself a 2-1 underdog for the notorious rematch. Many assumed that Tyson had taken Holyfield lightly and would not make the same mistake again. But when the bell rang Holyfield seemed to carry on from where he left off last time. He looked sharper than Tyson and radiated confidence. Once again he nullified Tyson by clinching and using his superior strength. In the second round Tyson got cut again and could clearly be seen complaining to Mills Lane about Holyfield's use of the head. Holyfield was in charge right and Tyson looked frustrated. In the third Tyson would have his famous meltdown and be disqualified after biting Holyfield twice - a hunk of Holyfield's ear ending up on the canvas.

Holyfield continued his remarkable renaissance when he avenged an earlier defeat by Michael Moorer with an eighth round TKO and then turned his attention to unification glory against rival champion Lennox Lewis. It was not to be though.

At 36, Holyfield suddenly seemed much slower than he had against Tyson a few years before and found the height and reach of Lewis too much. The first fight was outrageously scored a draw but everyone thought that Lewis had won. Holyfeld was somewhat better in the second bout but this time Lewis was given the official verdict on the cards.

Holyfield went 8-6-1 for the rest of his career, enduring medical suspensions and becoming something of a poster boy for those who can't seem to walk away from the sport. He did though, at the age of 45, challenge WBA champion Nikolai Valuev in 2008 only to get the wrong end of a close points verdict.

Michael Spinks won gold at the 1976 Montreal Olympics at middleweight and turned professional in 1977. Spinks would go on to become one of the greatest light-heavyweights in the history of the division. He won the WBA title against the talented and formidable Eddie Mustafa Muhammad and made ten defences. Spinks also unified the division by beating the WBC champion Dwight Muhammad Qawi on points in 1983. Qawi was a firecracker at 175 but Spinks boxed a smart fight to take a decision. Spinks was one of the most intelligent fighters ever to step inside a ring. He was a slow starter who would take time to figure his opponent out and then adjust to the style he was up against.

Spinks was tall at 6'2 and had a powerful right hand known as the Spinks Jinx. He could be unorthodox in the ring and adopt herky jerky movements to befuddle his opponent. In 1985, Spinks became the first light-heavyweight champion to successfully win the heavyweight title when he outpointed Larry Holmes over fifteen rounds. Spinks was a heavy underdog but Holmes underestimated him and was outhustled by the busier Spinks. Truth be told though, Spinks was never really a heavyweight. He was very lucky to get the decision in their rematch (most observers though Larry won the second fight) and then gave up his IBF belt because he wanted to fight Gerry Cooney rather than the IBF number one contender Tony Tucker. Cooney was inactive and past his best but he was a big name and a bigger payday. Spinks battered Cooney in five rounds.

It's a shame really that our last and unavoidably abiding memory of Spinks is his 40 second loss to Mike Tyson in 1988. Spinks was 33 by then and wore strapping on his legs in the ring because of his bad knees. If you had hooked the Spinks camp up to a lie detector machine I doubt any of them really believed he could beat Tyson. It was a fight they had to take though given that Spinks would be earning thirteen million dollars. Adjusted for inflation, thirteen million dollars in 1988 equates to around thirty million dollars today. You know what? I think even I'd be tempted to get beat up by Mike Tyson for thirty million dollars! It was the sort of money that Spinks and his team couldn't turn down.

It was really at light-heavyweight where we should remember Spinks. One interesting thing about his career is that he didn't bother with the cruiserweight division because at the time he moved up there was no one there to fight. However, a marketable and talented fighter at cruiserweight did emerge shortly after in the form of Evander Holyfield. So, we are going to propose a moment of alternative boxing history.

What if, after beating Larry Holmes, Spinks decided to go for the cruiserweight title to become a triple champion and a fight between him and Holyfield was made in late 86 or early 87. This fight was certainly spoken of a few times but there was never a point where it got anywhere near happening because Spinks had bigger fish to fry in the heavyweight division at the time. One could argue that 190 pounds would have suited Spinks very well. He would have had extra bulk and strength but not TOO much. He still would have had more of his old light-heavyweight speed.

People sometimes tend to assume (perhaps blinded by the Tyson-Spinks fight) that Holyfield would have destroyed Michael Spinks but this fight is a lot more competitive and hard to predict than you might think. Holyfield was an awesome fighting machine at cruiserweight but Ossie Ocasio did take him into the eleventh round of a title defence and Michael Spinks was a lot better than Ossie Ocasio.

Spinks also handled Dwight Muhammad Qawi much easier than Holyfield did in the first Holyfield v Qawi fight.

Michael Spinks would have been by far the most talented fighter Holyfield would have fought at that early point in his career. Holyfield would be stronger than Spinks but his ability to bully Spinks would be compromised by Spinks' right hand. I don't think Spinks could stop Holyfield but he could certainly keep him honest - especially if he landed a big shot early.

Spinks would look to fustrate Holyfield with his herky-jerky movement and not let Evander get set. Spinks would seek to catch Holyfield coming in with right-hands and Michael also had a really good defence and instinctive ability to evade punches. One could see a scenario where Holyfield showed Spinks a lot of respect and it became a surprisingly tricky and puzzling fight for him.

Spinks could also throw good fast combinations so this fight would not be one way traffic. This is a fight that Spinks could potentially win if he fought the perfect fight but you would probably, in the end, have to conjecture that the busier workrate of Evander and the pressure he would undoubtedly apply (Holyfield would be the aggressor in this fight - Spinks would most likely seek to fight on the back foot and counter) would be enough for him to edge the fight on the scorecards. I could see a long and surprisingly tactical fight which Holyfield wins a unanimous decision based on his higher output and harder punching. Spinks would definitely be a live underdog though and give Holyfield plenty to think about over the course of this fascinating matchup.

MUHAMMAD ALI
V
TEOFILO STEVENSON

Born Cassius Marcellus Clay, Muhammad Ali would transcend black stereotypes and boxing itself. When he converted to the Nation Of Islam he officially became public enemy number one. Ali refused to be drafted into the Vietnam war and was villified. Today most people look back and think he was probably right (however manipulated he may have been by the shrewd Nation of Islam) to protest against a terrible war - aware that many of the politicians and authority figures who went after him kept their own sons out of the draft. He was stripped of his title in his prime and endured a three year exile from boxing - the thing he loved most of all. Millions of dollars lost in earnings. That is perhaps the most extraordinary thing about this most extraordinary heavyweight. As brilliant as Ali was we probably never actually got to see him fight in his prime.

Ali had humble origins in Louisville, Kentucky, and got into boxing by chance. A skinny twelve year-old boy called Cassius Clay walked through the downstairs boxing gym of local policeman Joe Martin crying after attending a black function elsewhere in the building. Martin noticed him and asked what was wrong and the boy replied that his bike had been stolen and that he was going to "whup" whoever took it. "You'd better learn how to fight before you start challenging people," replied Martin. A legend was soon born and Clay, charismatic with incredibly fast hands, would become Olympic champion.

As a young professional, his brash interviews, poetry, and predictions were relatively new at the time, for boxing anyway. The young Ali quickly cottoned onto the rise in ticket sales that followed whenever he hyped up a fight - a trick he picked up after appearing on a radio show with a wrestler named Gorgeous George. George's flamboyant self-promotion was a big influence on Ali. His lifelong trainer, the amiable Italian-American Angelo Dundee, thought Ali was a "nut at first but soon realised there was something special about his new charge.

When Ali challenged Sonny Liston for the heavyweight championship no one expected him to win. The monstrous Liston was considered to be unbeatable and Ali was an 8 to 1 underdog who was expected to slip into obscurity after the ham like fists of the champion had inevitably exposed him. To the surprise of practically everyone, Ali proved a far trickier puzzle to solve than Liston had expected and the bamboozled and glum looking champion retired on his stool after eight rounds. The rematch saw Liston stopped in the first round by a chopping inside punch that appeared strangely innocuous. The two Liston bouts remain controversial and to this day some maintain the mob connected Liston threw the fights. Despite the speculation and theories there has never been any firm conclusive evidence to 100% confirm the suspicions.

Regardless, instead of the monosyllabic, complex, and somewhat intimidating Liston, a former prison convict who seemed to have everyone against him, the world suddenly and unexpectedly had a very different heavyweight champion. One who was media friendly (for Ali loved to talk), charming and - most importantly of all - funny. It would a while though for anyone to realise this and not until his 1970s comeback would he be truly accepted and loved. Ali's association with the Nation of Islam meant his popularity was modest to say the least when he won the title.

He made several defences of the heavyweight championship before his ban for refusing the draft, defeating contenders that included former champ Floyd Patterson, Cleveland Williams, Ernie Terrell, and Zora Folley. Ali was astonishingly quick for a heavyweight and could constantly move for 15 rounds if necessary. His stamina and reflexes were incredible. After his exile from the ring, Ali was not as quick or light on his feet as he used to be but he was bigger and stronger and his guile, courage, durability, and sheer force of will made him a formidable opponent indeed. He confirmed his greatness by besting a new decade of heavyweights and becoming champion again. After a few tune-ups, the stage is set for Ali to fight the new champion Joe Frazier.

Has there ever been a more epic sporting rivalry than the one between Ali and Frazier? Frazier is near the height of his powers and his incredible workrate and constant come-forward style earns him a 15 round points decision over Ali (who, lest we forget, is having only his third fight in four years). Ali finds himself somewhat in the wilderness now and is even upset by the then unheralded (but of course, as we would come to learn, very talented) Ken Norton before narrowly outpointing Norton in the rematch. If Ali had a bogeyman it was surely Ken Norton. Norton's style always gave him trouble.

After turning the tables on Norton, Ali then outpointed Joe Frazier in a 1974 rematch. Frazier was an ex-champion now, having been demolished by the apparently indestructible George Foreman. Ali boxed more in the second Frazier fight, using his movement to minimise the exchanges and frustrate Joe. The stage was now set for Foreman v Ali for the heavyweight championship. Could Ali regain the title at last?

The fight took place in Zaire (Don King promoted the fight and African dictator Mobutu Sese Seko agreed to stage it to promote his country) and remains one of the most incredible events in boxing history. Ali dubbed Foreman "The Mummy" and showed no sign of being worried about the prospect of taking on such a dangerous opponent. Foreman later remembers Ali talking to him constantly during their fight and mocking his punching power.

In was a new experience for the frightening and hugely powerful Foreman to have an opponent still standing after a few rounds let alone talking back to him. Ali shocked Foreman by throwing right-hand leads in the first round but he eventually retreated to the ropes - the "rope-a-dope" as it was dubbed. Foreman wailed away at him but Ali blocked, parried, swayed, and countered until Foreman was exhausted. A right-hand put the lumbering giant down for the count in the eight. Ali was champion again at 32.

After three defences, including a stoppage of the dangerous Ron Lyle, Ali met Joe Frazier for the third time in "The Thrilla in Manila". Although both men were past their primes they staged an extraordinary fight in intense heat. Ali was close to exhaustion when Frazier's trainer Eddie Futch refused to let his half-blind fighter come out for the last round. The bravery of both men was incredible. They were too proud to admit defeat and so effectively fought themselves to a standstill. Neither was ever the same again.

Ali made another six defences, including wins over the dangerous Earnie Shavers and Ken Norton in their rubber match. Ali was lucky to get the verdict against Norton and also Jimmy Young. It was a clear sign that he was nearing the end of an incredible career. Now in his mid-thirties, Ali was slower of hand and foot than he'd ever been but getting by on guts and guile. In 1978 Ali was outhustled by rookie pro Leon Spinks and lost on points. He beat Spinks in the rematch to regain the title and then retired. He should have left it at that but hubris and money led to two ill-fated twilight fights.

In 1980 he couldn't resist big money to fight the new heavyweight champion Larry Holmes. Now 38 and showing alarming signs of slurred speech and a wobbly gait, Ali was a shell of his former self and retired on his stool after ten rounds. He had one more fight in 1981, losing on points to Trevor Berbick. Neither fight should have been sanctioned or allowed to happen. Ali's greatness is secured by two title reigns and his mastery of the 60s and 70s generation of heavyweights. Both decades are considered to be strong ones in heavyweight history and so Ali's legacy is incredible - all the more so when one remembers that at the age of 27 he was banned for three years. It is no surprise that many regard him to be the greatest heavyweight of all time.

Teófilo Stevenson was a Cuban amateur boxer who competed from 1966 to 1986. He won three Olympic heavyweight gold medals in 1972, 1976, and 1980. Stevenson might even have won a fourth were it not for Cuba boycotting the 1984 Los Angeles games (due to the Soviet Union doing the same thing after the United States boycotted the Moscow Olympics because of the Soviet invasion of Afghanistan). As an amateur, Stevenson beat talented American fighters like Tony Tubbs, John Tate, and Michael Dokes - all of whom later won world titles in the professional ranks.

George Foreman said of Teófilo Stevenson in 1976 - "Stevenson is a champion in all kinds of ways. He has it all. Stevenson is about as better fighter as I've ever seen, professional or amateur. I haven't seen this much class and skill in the professional for a long time nor at the amateur. Stevenson would undoubtedly became champion of the world professionally if he decided to. He has the skill and qualification any time he wants to become champion of the world."

Given that Teófilo Stevenson's prime years coincided with Muhammad Ali being at the height of his fame in the 1970s, there was always a lot of speculation about a fight between them. The obvious problem though is that Stevenson was a Cuban and would have had to defect or get permission from Castro if he'd wanted to turn professional or fight Ali. Don King and Bob Arum allegedly both made attempts to persuade Teófilo Stevenson to turn professional and come to the United States but he never did. "What is a million dollars against eight million Cubans who love me?" said Stevenson.

Stevenson was 6'3 and weighed about 215 pounds. He had a very upright amateur style but he also had fast hands, nimble footwork, and a good defence. He could also punch too. Stevenson was exceptionally difficult to beat over three rounds but how would he have fared in a longer bout? The boxing authorities were perfectly happy to let Stevenson fight Ali in his professional debut and Castro apparently eventually gave his consent for the fighter to do this - even in the United States.

The sticking point though came over how many rounds such a fight would have taken place over. Ali wanted a traditional pro world title fight over fifteen rounds but Stevenson wanted to fight Ali in a special 'exhibition' bout over three or four rounds. Neither fighter was willing to grant the other's request and this, as much as anything, is why this fight never happened. A fight between Ali and Stevenson was the talk of boxing circles from as early as 1974. It would have most likely taken place around 1976 after Stevenson's further Olympic success.

Ali was definitely fading by 1976. He was 34 years-old and struggled in fights with Ken Norton and Jimmy Young that year. One could certainly argue that Ali should have retired for good after his third fight with Joe Frazier in 1975. That fight took a lot out of him and he was no spring chicken at 33 when it occurred. The question of who would have won between Ali and Stevenson obviously depends a lot on how many rounds they would have fought and in which year. Let's say, as seemed most likely, the fight took place circa 1976 when Ali still had a little bit (but not much) left in the tank and Stevenson was a two time Olympic legend.

As for rounds, we must sanction this fight as a title fight and that means fifteen rounds. It had to have been a real fight because otherwise it would have been nothing more than a glorified charity exhibition. So who would have won? It's easy to see the purposeful Stevenson taking the early rounds here as Ali clowns and plays to the crowd. Ali would most likely go to the ropes too and let Stevenson tire himself out.

Though Stevenson can punch the chances of a knockout for the Cuban are close to zero. Ali had one of the greatest chins in heavyweight history. If Foreman, Shavers, Liston, and Frazier couldn't knock out Ali how is Teófilo Stevenson supposed to do that? Stevenson would be competitive but after several rounds he would begin to tire and Ali would take control. The most likely outcome here is a late stoppage for Ali when Stevenson becomes fatigued due to his lack of professional experience.

Ali was used to fighting for fifteen rounds but Stevenson was not. This fight would certainly be interesting early but it's impossible to see how an amateur boxer, even one as great as Teófilo Stevenson, could beat Muhammad Ali - even the faded 76 version of Ali - in a fifteen round professional fight.

ROY JONES JR
V
NIGEL BENN

Roy Jones Jr was the greatest boxer of his generation. He won world titles in four different weight classes from middleweight to heavyweight and was unbeatable in his prime. The great shame of his career is that he fought well into the veteran phase and eventually picked up a number of losses against fighters he would have beaten easily in his prime. Had he retired after beating John Ruiz for the heavyweight title then there is a good chance that we would be talking about him as arguably the greatest fighter of all time - or certainly in the top ten.

Jones undoubtedly tarnished his reputation by fighting on for too long and picking up a raft of losses. You might say this is unfair and you'd be right about that because Jones should be judged on his prime years but that's the way it goes sometimes. When people think of Jones Jr now they struggle to shake off memories of him being kayoed by Antonio Tarver and Glen Johnson or dominated by Joe Calzaghe. Jones was past his best by the time these fights arrived.

The knock against Jones is that he carefully selected his opponents and avoided dangerous challenges but Jones couldn't really be blamed for the fact that he didn't fight in a more challenging era. There was no Thomas Hearns, Marvin Hagler, or Michael Spinks for Jones to fight. Jones spent most of his career at light-heavyweight but the 175 division was fairly mediocre at the time. That is obviously not the fault of Roy. All he could do was beat the contenders thrown at him by the alphabet bodies.

Jones did though beat all time greats in Bernard Hopkins and James Toney and also unify the world light-heavyweight titles. Jones never fought his only plausible 175 rival Dariusz Michalczewski but then does anyone really think that Michalczewski would have beaten a prime Roy Jones anyway? Michalczewski was a strong and competent fighter who had a good run as the WBO champion but he wouldn't have landed a glove on a primes Jones. I can tell you exactly how a Jones v Michalczewski fight would have gone. It would have gone just like most of Roy's other light-heavyweight fights! Roy would have won a dull points decision.

Jones didn't fight Michalczewski because he didn't want to go to Germany. You can hardly blame Roy for this given his experience of being robbed at the Olympics and the rather dodgy reputation of German boxing at the time - look at the Sven Ottke v Robin Reid fight for example, one of the most corrupt fights in memory. Michalczewski, for his part, didn't especially want to go to the United States to fight Roy because he was making a fortune fighting in Germany and saw no reason to travel to his rival's turf and give up home advantage. With neither man willing to compromise when it came to a venue this fight simply never got made.

Jones was a rather unique fighter in that he nothing he did conformed to the textbook of boxing. He rarely jabbed and kept his arms down low. Jones got by on his tremendous reflexes - which made him lightning quick and able to evade his opponent's punches. He was not known as a puncher but he could certainly hurt people when he wanted to. He finished Virgil Hill with a single body shot and poleaxed Montell Griffin in the first round of their rematch. Jones was unbeatable until his ill advised move back to light-heavyweight after beating John Ruiz for the WBA heavyweight title. After that he was mortal - and getting old. It was sad to see getting knocked out and dominated by fighters he would once have beaten easily.

Though Jones spent the longest part of his career at light-heavyweight he was at his best in the super-middleweight division. Jones seemed to be at his most destructive at 168 pounds. Sturdy fighters known for their durability like Vinnie Pazienza and Tony Thornton were brutally taken apart by Jones. The main problem anyone faced when in the ring with Jones was his incredible speed. His punches came so quickly that it was often very difficult to do anything about them. There was a swagger and sense of

invincibility to Jones in his prime. He was truly a remarkable
fighter. The only blemish on the record of the prime Jones was
a DQ loss to Montell Griffin in a fight Jones was winning.
Griffin was hit while on one knee. In the rematch Jones
destroyed Griffin in the first round.

Nigel Benn was one of the most entertaining and
charismatic British boxers of the modern era. In the eighties
and nineties he became a two time world champion at
different weights and had memorable encounters in the ring
against the likes of Doug Dewitt, Michael Watson, Chris
Eubank, Iran Barkley, Henry Wharton, and, tragically, Gerald
McClellan. His life outside the ring was every bit as colourful.
Benn admitted to being a tearaway as he grew up with no real
sense of direction. The only thing he was really good at was
fighting. After leaving school at an early age and spending time
on the dole, Benn was persuaded by his mother to join the
army. Another brother was already serving with First
Battalion, Royal Regiment of Fusiliers.

The army soon learned that they had a natural boxer on
their hands and doors started to open up to a possible future
in the ring. Benn served in Cyprus, Germany, and did a couple
of Tours Of Duty in Northern Ireland. "I don't think fear is an
emotion I will ever have after Northern Ireland," said Benn.
Benn initially left the army with no plans to box as a career. He
considered a role in a plan to rob a security van (!) and lived
on £38 a week dole money with his young family. A visit to
West Ham Boys Amateur Boxing Club set him back on course.
Benn was sensational when he turned professional. He was
sort of like a British middleweight version of Mike Tyson and
soon compiled a raft of knockout wins.

His first defeat, to Michael Watson, made Benn to go
'back to basics'. Benn punched himself out against Watson and
was stopped in the sixth round. The defeat actually made him
a better fighter. Benn said he was becoming too mixed up with
the showbusiness/hype side of boxing and needed to start
again. He headed for the Fifth Street Gym in Miami where
American boxers gave him severe workouts and sparring
sessions. Benn fought in the US for a period and beat tough
customers like Jorge Amparo, Jose Quinones and Sanderline

Williams in relative obscurity. He then beat Doug Dewitt in a tough up and down encounter to win the WBO Middleweight Championship.

Benn was stopped by Chris Eubank in their first fight in a classic encounter. Back in those days live boxing was a fixture on ITV and millions of people would tune in to watch the fights between Britain's 'Three Kings' - Benn, Eubank, and Watson. Benn said that he never felt quite the same after a bruising encounter with Henry Wharton in 1994. There was another bout with Eubank (the rematch between Benn and Eubank was a draw that most people thought Benn won) and, of course, the tragic encounter with Gerald McClellan.

McClellan was Don King's latest superstar. The 'G-Man' was headed for a planned superfight with Roy Jones and Benn was just a stepping stone. An easy to hit British boxer who was probably just on the way down. Benn confounded the critics by stopping McClellan in an extraordinary, brutal encounter but his greatest triumph turned into his biggest nightmare when McClellan collapsed and suffered a brain injury. McClellan was left blind and deaf. It was a brutal fight and ultimately a tragic night. Benn had nearly been knocked out in the first round when McClellan knocked him through the ropes. A glassy eyed Benn was actually pushed back into the ring by a TV commentary team. Though dazed and wobbly, Benn somehow fought back and survived the round. It was typical Nigel Benn. He would just keep swinging and never give up.

Benn made nine defences of the WBC super-middleweight championship and in his career beat the likes of Iran Barkley, Gerald McClellan, Doug DeWitt, and Robbie Sims. As we have noted, Benn was also very unlucky not have a win in the rematch against Eubank on his slate. Three of Benn's losses came when he was past his prime. Benn was ferocious puncher and as tough as old boots. At his very best he was capable of giving anyone a tough and rough night. Benn was the most exciting British fighter of his era.

The time to make a Jones v Benn fight was circa 1994/early 1995 when both were fighting at 168 pounds. For some reason or other, chiefly boxing politics, Jones and Benn never actually met in the ring. Jones was always wary of fighting abroad after his experience at the Olympics in South Korea (where he was robbed by corrupt officials) and Benn's association with Don King was another possible stumbling block.

Benn said that Jones would have been his ultimate challenge although he also suggested at one point he was relieved the fight didn't happen. It seems to be the case that this fight never got made because neither fighter was especially obsessed by it. Jones never went out of his way to get a fight with Benn and Benn wasn't too fussed either about fighting Jones. These two boxers were both content to avoid one another.

Anyway, who would have won had these two ever climbed into the ring together? Roy Jones would clearly start as a prohibitive favourite in this fight. He is faster than Benn, bigger than Benn, and a much better natural boxer than Benn. Jones would have a lot of obvious advantages in this fight. Jones would also be able to dictate the tempo from the outside and try and pick Benn off at arm's length. Jones was sort of like a snake charmer in the way he would dangle a low lazy left hand in front of his opponent as he waited for an opportunity to strike.

There is no major secret concerning what Benn would have to do to win this fight. Benn would have to get inside and try and land something big. Benn could hurt anyone if he hit them and he was a great finisher. If he got Jones going he'd jump all over him. Unfortunately though for Nigel that would be easier said than done. Nigel would have to fight a very patient fight and take his share of shots from Jones. Benn's best chance would be to get through the first half of the fight and then try to crank up the pressure.

In the sad last phase of the career of Roy Jones he seemed to have something of a glass chin. Antonio Tarver, Danny Green, Glen Johnson, Denis Lebedev, and Enzo Maccarinelli all knocked him out. However, these men were not really fighting the real Roy Jones. He had a bit left when he fought Tarver but Jones was clearly not the same after coming back down to 175 from heavyweight. Green, Denis Lebedev, and Enzo Maccarinelli all fought a washed up shell of

Roy Jones.

Still, the perception - retrospective in nature - remains that Jones must have this glass jaw all along and would therefore have potentially been vulnerable against a notorious puncher like Nigel Benn. The problem with this theory though is that even if it is true and Roy was packing glass all along, the lightning reflexes of the prime Jones meant that he rarely got hit!

This is why we never saw the prime Roy Jones get knocked out in the same way that the old Roy Jones did. The young Roy Jones was simply too fast to hit. He was knocked down by Lou Del Valle in a 175 pound world title defence but that's about it. And Jones got back to his feet and won the fight easily. A big haymaker from Nigel, if such a punch landed, would clearly have the potential to hurt Roy but the chances of such a punch landing seem questionable at best.

Nigel's best strategy in this fight would be to go to the body and try and rough Roy up. He'd have to deny Roy the space to work as much as he could because Roy is clearly going to beat Benn on the outside with his faster hands. Even this strategy is not guaranteed to work though because Roy was no slouch on the inside either. He quite enjoyed laying on the ropes and using his quick hands to counter his opponent with combinations to the head and body. This is why Roy Jones was such a great fighter in his prime. He could beat people in various different ways.

This fight would certainly be entertaining and Nigel would assuredly have given it a real go but it's hard to see how he could have beaten a prime Roy Jones given the huge advantage in speed and natural boxing ability that Jones would enjoy. The best guess of this fantasy fight is that Jones would have stopped a tiring Nigel Benn somewhere in the latter half of the fight after Nigel began to feel the effects from the accumulation of all the punches that Roy landed early. Jones is the clear pick here although Benn could never be completely discounted given his ability to turn any fight on its head with a big punch and his incredible never say die spirit.

DAVID TUA
V
MIKE TYSON

David Tua was born in Samoa and fought out of New Zealand. He won a Bronze medal at the1992 Olympics in Barcelona. That same year he turned professional and soon developed a reputation as an exciting knockout artist and prospect. In 1996, Tua stole the show on a bill featuring heavyweight prospects when he kayoed John Ruiz in a matter of seconds. Ruiz later went on to become a world champion and fight in numerous title bouts.

Tua then beat the tough Oleg Maskaev before being matched with another prospect named Ike Ibeabuchi. Ibeabuchi was an unbeaten Nigerian heavyweight based in America. He looked a lot like Sonny Liston and fought a bit like him too. Tua's fight with Ibeabuchi was an all action slugfest in which an astonishing amount of punches were thrown. Amazingly, these two granite jawed fighters took everything the other had to offer and the fight went to the cards. Tua felt he had won but Ibeabuchi got the nod.

Three fights later Ike Ibeabuchi kayoed the normally elusive Chris Byrd in the fifth round and seemed to be the next big thing in the division but the troubled fighter was incarcerated for sexual assault and never fought again. As for Tua, he dusted himself down and put together a winning streak. Because he had a high ranking and was due a title shot his handlers didn't take too many risks but he did stop future champion Hasim Rahman in the tenth round of their 1998 fight.

Tua was short for a heavyweight at 5'10 but he was built like a tank and impossible to hurt. He had a truly great chin. Tua's was famous for his left-hook. He was a fearsome puncher when this signature hook landed. Tua's weakness was that he could be outboxed. If you were managing Tua you'd much rather put him in the ring with an aggressive puncher than a slick mover. Tua wasn't exactly light on his feet and would plod after his opponents. Despite his short stature he could weigh as much as 250 in the ring. He was just a very powerful and bulky man - simply not very tall.

Tua got his title shot against Lennox Lewis in 2000. Many actually tipped him to win the fight but he found the size, reach, and boxing ability of Lewis too much to cope with. Lewis won a lopsided decision. Tua never got another title shot. Two fights later he was outpointed by the slippery Chris Byrd. Tua had good wins against Michael Moorer and Fres Oquendo and fought a draw with his old rival Hasim Rahman but he was never a major factor in the division again. His new promoter Cedric Kushner tried to get him a fight with Wladimir Klitschko but this never came off. Tua's only other losses came at the end of his career when he was well past his best.

When Tua first burst onto the scene, Mike Tyson was serving a ban for biting evander Holyfield's ear in their rematch. The opponent for Tyson's 1999 comeback was Frans Botha, a South African heavyweight known as The White Buffalo. Botha could box and was a tough customer but he wasn't much of a puncher and so wasn't expected to pose too many problems for Tyson. Botha had beaten Axel Schulz for the vacant IBF title in 1995 but was then stripped when he tested positive for the steroid nandrolone. Botha claimed he innocently took the drug when being treated for an arm injury. When he fought Michael Moorer for the title in his next fight he was stopped in the last round.

The fight with Botha was Tyson at his worst save for the ending. Botha outboxed the rust strewn Tyson with embarrassing ease and the former champion reacted by trying to break the South African's arm no less than three times, or forcibly twist it at least. The first incident of this provoked an after the bell reaction from Botha and threatened a mass brawl from either camp as the boxers were forcibly separated. Tyson was supposed to be on his best behaviour that night but he didn't seem to have changed his ways an awful lot. Botha continued to outbox him with the greatest threat from Tyson coming to the South African's arms rather than his chin. When Tyson did finally connect with a cruncher in the fifth Botha went down and failed to beat the count. The punch masked what had been a dire showing from Tyson. If he wanted another title shot he would have to sharpen up considerably.

In February, the now 32 year-old Tyson was sentenced to two years in a Maryland prison for "a dramatic example, a tragic example of potentially lethal road rage." Given that he still owed millions in taxes and $6 million to former trainer Kevin Rooney the last thing Tyson needed was to be away from his main source of income - boxing. Tyson had now acquired the services of the shrewd and respected Shelly Finkel as his manager but even Finkel's testimony couldn't keep Tyson out of jail. It didn't help Tyson's cause that the victims were elder citizens. All it did was further cement the image of him as a bully and a thug. He was out by the end of the year and an opponent for the second comeback fight of his THIRD comeback odyssey was sought.

One name in the frame was none other than Buster Douglas. Buster had made a comeback in the mid-nineties, ostensibly for health reasons. After retiring in the wake of his dismal surrender to Holyfield, Douglas had ballooned to 400 pounds and fell into a diabetic coma. The comeback didn't amount to much though and came to an abrupt end when the white heavyweight hopeful Lou Savarese stopped him in the first round. Buster fought a few no names as he angled for a fight against the brilliant light-heavyweight Roy Jones Jr but Tyson's brains trust decided against fighting him in the end. Buster was said to weigh 300 pounds and with his punch resistance gone even a faded 32 year-old Tyson versus the 1999 version of Douglas would have been legalised manslaughter.

Tyson's team chose 34 year-old Orlin Norris instead. Norris was a respected boxer with a good curriculum vitae. He was the former WBA cruiserweight champion and in two campaigns at heavyweight had beaten Oliver McCall, Renaldo Snipes, Greg Page and avenged a loss against Tony Tucker (albeit a Tucker who had seen better days come the rematch). Henry Akinwande had soundly outpointed Norris in his most recent heavyweight campaign but then the 6'8 Akinwande was a class boxer and had huge size and reach advantages over the 5'10 Norris. In his last bout before meeting Tyson, Norris had whacked out the British heavyweight prospect Pele Reid in one round. It was felt that if Tyson boxed as poorly as he did against Botha then the crafty Norris, a good fluid boxer with quick hands, would have a reasonable chance of boxing his way to a points decision.

Norris did well enough in the first round, remaining calm when Tyson tried to rush him. Orlin even started to get his jab going and used his footwork to circle away from Tyson's left hook. As the first round ended, Tyson hit Norris after the bell. It wasn't the most devastating punch Tyson had ever thrown and came across as more of a petulant cheap shot than anything. He had two points deducted as the crowd booed Brownsville's most famous pantomime villain. Norris went down on his back in delayed fashion after the punch and then looked somewhat sheepish and got back up again to walk back to his corner. Tyson (now trained by Tommy Brooks) came out for the second to find Norris still on his stool. He had quit, claiming a knee injury (which was later verified) as a result of going down at the end of the first round. The fight was ruled no-contest and Tyson echoed the sentiments of everyone who had tuned in. "I'm tired of this s***."

Tyson's purse was temporarily withheld from the bout but then handed over when it proved impossible to ascertain whether the punch just after the bell was purposefully malicious. Orlin Norris and his management salivated at the expected rematch payday they would collect but Tyson decided to pull the rug out from under them and take his increasingly obstreperous act on the road. He announced (to the ire of Norris, who launched an unsuccessful legal challenge once he realised his rematch hopes were dust) that he would travel across the Atlantic to take on the British champion Julius Francis in Manchester. The fight made a lot of sense as fans (and the generally curious) were eager to see Tyson in the flesh and so there was money to be made. It would also get Tyson out of the United States where the commissions were (understandably) starting to grow more than a little weary of the carnage and confusion he seemed to bring to any event.

The fight with Francis was a gross mismatch but no one could deny that the likeable 35 year-old Julius, a journeyman who had lost seven fights since taking up boxing in his late twenties, at least deserved a decent twilight payday for all of his toil. Francis managed to get the Tyson fight through a three fight winning streak that brought victories over his domestic rivals Pele Reid, Scott Welch and the promising Danny Williams. Tyson's main concern was getting into the country. After protests and much debate, the British Home Secretary decided that Tyson should be allowed in to fight.

It was more of an event than a sporting contest. Julius enjoyed his fifteen minutes of fame and took up an offer to have the soles of his boxing shoes sponsored for £20,000. The light-hitting Francis lacked the power to keep Tyson at bay and was knocked down five times before the referee called a halt in the second round. The exercise hadn't proved an awful lot in terms of Tyson's status as a contender but it did prove that he could draw a crowd in Europe.

Five months later Tyson was back in the United Kingdom to meet more protests as he took on the big Texan Lou Savarese in Glasgow. The pair were supposed to meet in Milan but when Tyson had to attend the funeral of a friend and needed more time to train the fight was moved to Scotland. Glasgow, like Manchester, was eager to see Tyson and there was plenty of money to made for Iron Mike and his British promoter Frank Warren. Only this time the trip took on the aura of a bad nightmare and ensured that Tyson would not fight in the British Isles again.

Savarese seemed on the face of it to be a reasonable choice of opponent. He was 6'5 and had wins over Buster Mathis Jr and Lance Whitaker. He stopped the comebacking Buster Douglas in the first round of a 1998 fight and had gone the distance with George Foreman and Michael Grant in losses. At the very least he might test Tyson's stamina. Tyson arrived by Concorde and avoided the press at Heathrow airport.

Tyson was off the mood-altering prescription drug Zoloft and seemed like a man possessed at a rain sodden

Hampden Park. The promoter Frank Warren sported an obvious eye injury at this time and there were heavy rumours that Tyson had been responsible after an altercation. Tyson later claimed in his autobiography that he was high when he entered the ring this night and his crazed behaviour suggests he wasn't lying. By now Tyson was a habitual user of drugs but evaded being caught in drug tests by using someone else's urine. He went after Savarese like a madman and dropped him with practically the first punch. When Savarese got up, Tyson went in for the kill and when the referee John Coyle tried to stop the fight he seemed oblivious to him and carried on pounding away on Lou. Coyle was then knocked down himself in the confusion and had to jump again to try and stop the fight for a second time while the cornermen entered the ring to prize them apart.

The fight was over at 38 seconds of the first round and Tyson immediately began ranting at Lennox Lewis (now the unified champion after beating Evander Holyfield) when interviewed by Showtime. "I was gonna rip his heart out. I'm the best ever. I'm the most brutal and vicious, the most ruthless champion there has ever been. No one can stop me. Lennox is a conqueror? No! He's no Alexander! I'm Alexander! I'm the best ever. I'm Sonny Liston. I'm Jack Dempsey. There's never been anyone like me. I'm from their cloth. There is no one who can match me. My style is impetuous, my defense is impregnable, and I'm just ferocious. I want your heart! I want to eat his children! Praise to Allah." Tyson was retrospectively fined $187,500 by the British Boxing Board of Control for misconduct. He'd probably lost more than that down the back of his sofa.

"One minute I'm robbing a dope house," reflected a maudlin Tyson, musing on his past and rapid rise to fame. "Next minute I'm the youngest heavyweight champion of the world. I'm only 20, 19, with a lot of money. Who am I? What am I? I don't even know who I am. I'm just a dumb child who's being abused and robbed by lawyers. I'm just a dumb pugnacious fool. I'm just a fool who thinks he's someone. Then you tell me I should be responsible. I've been a prima-donna. I was taken care of since I was 13. That's why I am the way I am today. I was spoiled, like a brat. I had anything I wanted. That's crazy to be that way all your life. Everybody's taking care of you, but manipulating you at the same time. Very few people have a life like that. Most people have to work like slaves their whole lives. I've never had a job in my life. What I know how to do is hurt big, tough men — in the street and off."

Tyson's last fight of 2000 was much anticipated although probably not for the right reasons. His opponent would be Andrew Golota, the "Foul Pole" as the American boxing press sometimes dubbed him. Golota was a huge white heavyweight who shot to prominence when he twice battered Riddick Bowe and then threw victory away when he was disqualified for low-blows in the last rounds. All Golota had to do to beat Bowe was box his way through to the end but he seemed to have a self-destructive lack of discipline that reminded many of Tyson. Earlier in his career Golota had also bitten an opponent. The prospect of him meeting Tyson had many anticipating a WWE style anything goes brawl. But Golota, despite his fearsome reputation, had a fragile psyche. He folded in one round in a 1997 title fight with Lennox Lewis and seemed to be beating overhyped prospect Michael Grant handily when he quit in the last round of a 1999 contest. His fight with Tyson at The Palace, Auburn Hills, Michigan, proved to be another bizarre night in the careers of both men.

Tyson came out fast in aggressive fashion and Golota immediately looked somewhat flustered and uncomfortable. Tyson looked better than he had done for a long time in the first round. He slipped punches and countered well. The old speed that the 1980s Tyson possessed in abundance was never going to return but at least he was showing some upper-body movement again at last. Golota went down from a big right-hand and ended the round with a cut. Golota would later claim that he was disoriented and injured after being butted - which was somewhat ironic given Tyson's complaints about Holyfield.

Despite his huge size advantage, Golota couldn't seem to get to grips with Tyson and looked like a novice golden glover trying to fend off the attacks. Between the second and third rounds Golota told his corner he didn't want to continue. His trainer Al Certo was gobsmacked and clearly furious. Golota was jeered as he left the ring and his purse was withheld. He was branded a coward but those quick to judge had to take back their scorn when it was later established that Golota had suffered a concussion, a fractured left cheekbone and a herniated disc. What had been an impressive performance by Tyson was scratched from TKO3 to No-Contest when he tested positive for marijuana. By this stage of his career no one was hugely surprised by anything that happened to him anymore. Tyson's boxing license in Michigan was suspended for three months.

The main goal of Team Tyson in 2001 was to get a big money title fight with Lennox Lewis. To this end, Tyson signed to fight top ten contender David Izon in May. But in April, a sloppy Lewis didn't bother to train or travel early to acclimatise in a defence against Hasim Rahman in Johannesburg and was stopped in the fifth round. Tyson and Shelly Finkel immediately lost interest in Izon and started to lobby for a fight with Rahman but Rahman was tied to a rematch clause with Lewis despite attempts by Don King to make a Rahman v Izon fight. It was quite a merry-go-round. The Rahman v Lewis rematch was set for november and in order to keep busy and earn more much needed money, Tyson and his team signed to fight the Dane Brian Nielsen in Copenhagen on September the 8th.

While he began training for the fight, Tyson was accused of sexual assault in the California resort town of Big Bear City. Nothing came of the charges but it was another reminder of how trouble and suspicion seemed to dog him at every turn. Despite his 62-1 record, Brian Nielsen was not taken very seriously by the boxing world at large. The pudgy Dane had feasted on geriatric names that had seen better days (Tim Witherspoon, Bonecrusher Smith, Tony Tubbs etc) and been the recipient of a highly questionable home advantage points decision over the ancient Larry Holmes in 1997. There was too the farce of him picking up the dubious IBO championship and gunning for Rocky Marciano's 49-0 record. It was all too comical for words and boxing historians everywhere were probably relieved or simply amused when an exhausted

Nielson collapsed to a tenth round loss to someone called Dicky Ryan in the bout that was supposed to make history.

Nielson had won thirteen straight since the Ryan fight but he was merely a fringe contender. He might scrape into a very fallow top twenty but that was about it. His marketability stemmed from him being a big fish in a small pond. Tyson was paid $5 million to travel to Denmark to fight Nielson and he certainly lived it large, treating the trip as more of a holiday than anything serious. Come fight night, a grossly out of shape Tyson weighed in at a shade under 240 pounds. Neilson was even more bloated at a whopping 260 pounds.

The fight had all the excitement and drama of a man fighting a paper bag. Nielson ambled onto the ropes and allowed a patently out of condition Tyson to thump away at him as if the Dane was a heavybag. A combination sent Nielson down in the third but the big European managed to clinch enough to give the crowd a few more rounds of increasingly desperate slow motion entertainment. Nielson, his left eye shut, retired on his stool at the end of the sixth round and Tyson was declared a TKO winner. A month later, Lennox Lewis regained his world title with a spectacular fourth round knockout of Hasim Rahman in their rematch. The decks were now clearing for Tyson versus Lewis in what was likely to be Tyson's last hurrah.

Despite the fact that Tyson looked dreadful against Nielson, Lewis v Tyson was projected to be the biggest fight in boxing history. Tyson's increasingly unstable and erratic behaviour was of course, distasteful as it was, a big part of the appeal. The fight was complicated to arrange because Lewis was with HBO and Tyson with Showtime and both networks were adamant they should have exclusive rights. In the end the money made everyone willing to compromise just enough to get the deal done. They would, in effect, share the fight.

At a press conference in New York to officially announce the fight Tyson strolled out on stage to wait for Lewis and then apparently tried to attack him when a bemused Lewis entered with a bodyguard who seemed to try and push Tyson back. Their respective entourages engaged in a mass brawl and somewhere in the midst of all the chaos Tyson bit Lewis on the leg. It was hard to believe that the two boxers had sparred as unknown amateurs in the early eighties and had always respected each other. Cus D'Amato is said to have predicted they would one day meet for the world championship.

The fight was supposed to take place in Las Vegas but the Nevada State Athletic Commission voted 4-1 to deny Tyson a licence and it was Memphis that coughed up the big site fee to get the fight. Both men were to be paid a guaranteed $17.5 million. It was the highest-grossing event in pay-per-view history, generating $106.9 million from 1.95 million buys in the United States. Tyson didn't endear himself to anyone with his team for the fight, most notably Panama Lewis, a man forever shamed for the despicable and ultimately tragic act of removing the padding from the gloves of Luis Resto when he fought a young fighter named Billy Collins years ago. Lewis had also been involved in a "mysterious bottle" incident when Aaron Pryor fought Alexis Arguello.

Tyson's other unlovable camp member was Steve "Crocodile" Fitch, an obnoxious cheerleader who wore combat fatigues and went around shouting a lot until everyone wanted to strangle him. "Crocodile is back from the swamp," said Lewis' trainer Emanuel Steward. "And then they went to the swamp and got Panama Lewis. That's too bad because it brings things back in the direction of it being a freak show. We have a big enough problem with Mike's reputation and integrity without bringing in Panama Lewis. I don't want Panama Lewis or Crocodile anywhere near the ring on Saturday night because, when they realize that Mike is about to get knocked out, they could resort to anything."

Meanwhile, Tyson's bizarre behaviour reached new disturbing lows when he overheard a journalist suggest he should be put in a straightjacket and launched into a profanity laced tirade while appearing to be on the cusp of tears. His interviews in training camp were frequently obscene and incoherent. Tyson seemed to be in meltdown. Strange as it seems in hindsight, Lewis was only a 2-1 favourite and many liked the chances of a Tyson victory. Memories perhaps of the savage assaults on Savarese and Golota were fresh in the mind but if the Nielson fight proved anything it was that Tyson's stamina was highly suspect these days.

He could still punch but the volume and speed had waned over the years and it was doubtful that Tyson could fight several hard competitive rounds with a top heavyweight now. Paradoxically, while Tyson was arguably 15 years removed from his prime, Lewis had been a late bloomer and at 35 seemed to be only a few years ahead of his peak. The highly rated Tyson-esque New Zealand slugger David Tua had failed to land a glove on Lewis in their title fight a few years before so it was hard to see how Tyson, at this advanced stage of his career, was likely to do much better.

Come fight night the pair were separated in the by yellow jacketed security guards lest there should be any last minute Tyson shenanigans. There was no staredown - the boxers getting their instructions in the dressing room beforehand. Tyson (lighter than in was in Denmark but still looking somewhat overweight at 234) started fast, looking for an early kayo but Lewis was calm and tied the shorter man up before hammering in some uppercuts to show he wouldn't be bullied. Tyson missed wildly with a hook and Lewis leaned down on Tyson, using his greater weight and strength. Tyson showed a flash of the old Tyson with a hook off the jab but Lewis landed a right late in the round as Tyson stooped low. It was a fairly even round but Tyson's attacking intent meant he probably deserved it by a whisker. "If you see how bad he looks you'd be surprised," Steward told Lewis in the corner.

Lewis landed a big uppercut early in the second and started to get his jab working. Lewis was also using his strength to shove Tyson back - similar to the tactics Evander Holyfield had used to negate Tyson's offensive style. Lewis was warned by the referee Eddie Cotton for holding but he was also starting to time the oncoming Tyson with uppercuts. Tyson couldn't get inside and close the distance and as the pace lulled Lewis began to dominate from the outside.

In the third Lewis began to move more and outboxed Tyson from the outside. Tyson look discouraged although he did manage a flurry that had the crowd excited for a fleeting moment. But a jab cuts Tyson above the eye and his night becomes even more difficult. As the fourth round began, blood was visible on Tyson's face. Lewis landed a thumping right and started to impose himself more and more. He shoved Tyson back and landed a left-hook to the body as Iron Mike began to bleed from the nose. Lewis seemed to knock Tyson down with a right-hand but the referee Eddie Cotton ruled that Lewis had pushed him down as a toppling Tyson leaned forwards. Bizarrely, Cotton then took a point from a bemused Lewis. Manny Steward was furious at Lewis in the corner. "Get this mother***** out of here! The man is finished!"

After a brief surge from Tyson at the start of the fifth it was all Lewis again. Lewis seemed to hurt Tyson with a right-hook inside but Eddie Cotton warned him for hitting and holding and gave Tyson time to recover. Larry Merchant on HBO acidly commented that Lennox was fighting both Tyson and the referee. Lewis pot shots with the jab when they continue and at the bell Tyson's trainer Ronnie Shields implores him to throw more punches. But the sixth and seventh round are one-way traffic as Lewis starts to line up a patently exhausted Tyson with the right-hand and hit him at will.

Tyson came out fast in the eighth and threw a couple of thudding rights at the side of Lewis but it's too late. He walks onto a combination and his knees buckle. Eddie Cotton (erroneously) gives him a count and the end is nigh. A big slashing right ends the contest and Tyson fails to beat the ten count. It was - ultimately - a brutal mismatch and the most punishing defeat of Tyson's career. Tyson, as chaotic as the pre-fight nonsense had been, emerged with some respect from the last big pay-per-view event of his career. He had taken his beating like a man and after the fight he even displayed his tender side when he praised Lewis and wiped some blood from the face of his opponent. It was a small moment but a reminder of what a puzzle Tyson was. For a second he could have been the young teenage Tyson who would be polite and respectful and talk excitedly about old fight films.

Lewis was eager for a rematch for two salient reasons. (1) He knew he would win again and (2) it would be a big payday to take into retirement. Tyson needed the rematch for financial reasons but somehow he eventually let it slip from his grasp. He said he needed some tune-ups before he boxed Lewis again but at 36 it was probably not going to make much difference. Tyson divorced his wife Monica Turner in 2003 and filed for bankruptcy. Tyson's days of commanding huge fight purses were almost over so things looked bleak indeed.

In February he was back in Memphis with new trainer Freddie Roach to fight Clifford "The Black Rhino" Etienne for $5 million and speculation arose that if Tyson won then a summer rematch with Lewis might go ahead. Etienne began boxing late after time in prison and was a real prospect at one time after wins against Lamon Brewster and Lawrence Clay Bey but a loss to Fres Oquendo that saw Etienne down seven times had derailed his progress and introduced some realism into projections of how far he might go. In his only fight of note since then he had drawn with Tyson's old foe Frans Botha.

At 225, Tyson looked trimmer than he had done for a while but it was of course impossible to know if training or drugs had made him so fashionably slender. The fight lasted 49 seconds and Etienne's performance evoked memories of Bruce Seldon's meek surrender to Tyson in the nineties. He went down from the first solid punch that Tyson landed and while prostrate on the canvas seemed aware enough to take his gumshield out before resuming his prostrate form like an actor playing a death scene. Maybe Etienne just thought better of getting walloped again.

Tyson nearly signed to fight Oleg Maskaev on the undercard of Lennox Lewis' June title defence against Vitali Klitschko but legal troubles (alleged to come from Don King) scuppered the plan. It would have paved the way for Lewis v Tyson 2. Tyson's 2003 rapidly descended into cocaine madness. He got into trouble for beating up two autograph hunters and kicked Don King in the head during some vague attempt at settling the circuitous legal maze their association had created. Tyson was also accused of breaking a bone in the face of one of King's bodyguards.

A maudlin Tyson bared his soul in an interview relating to his financial woes although it was hard to feel sorry for a man who had blown $300 million by treating it like monopoly money. "I've got nowhere to live. I've been crashing with friends, literally sleeping in shelters. Unsavoury characters are giving me money and I'm taking it. I need it. The drug dealers, they sympathise with me. They see me as some sort of pathetic character ... I know I was a tough, bad-ass talking fighter, but I ain't no mob figure. I did my time for the rape. I paid my money to Las Vegas. I paid my dues. I ain't the same person I was when I bit that guy's ear off. If they don't have that extreme addict personality, you can never understand how a guy can blow 300 or 400 million dollars. If I have to live at the top of the world, I also have to live at the bottom of the ocean. I don't know how to live in the middle of life."

In July 2004, Tyson was finally back in the ring, this time in Louisville, Kentucky, to fight the unheralded 31-year-old British heavyweight Danny Williams. Williams was known as a wholehearted and competent fighter at domestic level in the United Kingdom but he had losses to Julius Francis and Michael Sprott on his record so Tyson, forgivably perhaps, wasn't taking him too seriously. Williams was installed as a 9-1 underdog against the now 38 year-old Tyson who, according to his autobiography, took drugs right before the fight.

Drugs or no drugs, Tyson nearly stopped Williams in the first. He landed some stinging punches and had the huge Londoner (all 265 pounds of him) wobbling and disorganised. Tyson however had torn a knee ligament through his exertions and a composed and determined Williams began to get on top, using his huge bulk to lean on Tyson and wear him down. Tyson was cut in the third from a stray elbow and received a low-blow. Danny had two points deducted for the fouls but the end for Tyson was not far off anyway.

Tyson's fighting spirit, sapped by years of abusing his body, seemed to wilt in the fourth. Williams began to pound Tyson with damaging punches and one could see that Tyson's stomach for combat had gone now after so many years in the squared circle. Tyson went down and looked completely exhausted. He failed to clamber up in time and Williams began to celebrate. Danny wouldn't have lasted a round against the 1986 version of Tyson but that version of Tyson only existed in fight films and scrapbooks now. It was the end of an era.

It has long been a sad tradition in boxing that great fighters and champions inevitably end careers losing to people they would have demolished in their prime. One thinks of Roy Jones Jr fighting on long after he should have retired and being knocked out by men he would have once beaten with one arm tied behind his back. Tyson would have one more ill-advised fight in June 2005 at the at MCI Center in Washington. His opponent was a little known 32 year-old Irish heavyweight named Kevin McBride.

McBride's 32–4–1 record included stoppage losses to Michael Murray, Louis Monaco, Axel Schulz and DaVarryl Williamson. He was the type of opponent the young Tyson would have feasted on in spectacular fashion but the fight would finally confirm that Tyson had absolutely nothing left. The bout featured more fouling and shoving than punching and Tyson - obviously out of condition and in no state to be in a boxing ring - was penalised for a head-butt. Tyson's old desperate trick of trying to twist his opponent's arm was also back. It was desperate stuff.

McBride, who weighed a preposterous 271 pounds, weathered the rough stuff and took Tyson's best shots when the faded slugger could land one. Tyson's handspeed was so diminished now that even his vaunted power seemed absent. At the end of the sixth, Tyson was shoved to the canvas and looked incapable of getting back up. He was on the verge of exhaustion. He retired on his stool before the seventh round and Kevin McBride had a victory, albeit a hollow largely meaningless one, over the worn out shell of what had once been one of the most exciting heavyweights to ever climb between the ropes. "I don't have the guts to stay in the sport anymore," Tyson said after the fight. "I most likely won't fight anymore. I won't disrespect the sport by losing to a fighter of this calibre." Sixteen days later Tyson announced his retirement.

Throughout this last up and down phase of Tyson's career there was a lot of talk about a Tyson v Tua fight. It seemed like a natural. Two big punchers with similar styles. Tua was desperate for the Tyson fight and called out Tyson more than once. Sure, it was the payday which motivated him but he was also convinced he could beat this faded version of Tyson. Tua v Tyson was a fight that could have been made from 1999 until the end of Tyson's career but it never happened in the end. The main reason it never happened is probably that Tyson's camp thought was too dangerous. They didn't want to jepordise a title shot by fighting anyone TOO tough.

Anyway, let's pretend that things had turned out differently and Tyson and Tua had fought in 2001. Who would have won? While I would have no hesitation in picking a prime Tyson to beat Tua handily I don't think the 2001 version of Tyson would enjoy fighting Tua at all. Tua had a fantastic chin and although Tyson was a big puncher even in his declining years it's hard to see him knocking out Tua. The main problem Tyson would face in this fight was that by 2001 he could only fight at a fast pace for three or four rounds. That spells disaster against Tua - a fighter who carried his knockout power into the late rounds.

I can picture a scenario where Tua has to take a few bombs early on but stops a fatigued Tyson late in the fight. It would certainly be an entertaining fight with plenty of big punches, mauling, and inside action. Ultimately, I just don't think the 2001 version of Tyson had enough left in the tank to go hammer and tongs with Tua for twelve hard rounds and so you'd have to pick Tua to come out on top. Tua wanted the fight because he knew Tyson was over the hill and fans wanted the fight because they had images of the young Tyson in their head and liked the idea of him engaging in a war with Tua. Sadly though that version of Tyson only resided in the past. Iron Mike was simply a memory.

FLOYD MAYWEATHER JR
V
PRINCE NASEEM HAMED

Floyd Mayweather Jr is the most celebrated boxer of the modern era. He won 15 major world championships from super featherweight to light middleweight and retired undefeated with a 50-0 record. He won his first world title at junior-lightweight but won world titles all the way to junior-middleweight in the end. He beat Diego Corrales, Zab Judah, Oscar De La Hoya, Manny Pacquiao, Ricky Hatton, Juan Manuel Márquez, Miguel Cotto, Canelo Álvarez, Shane Mosley, José Luis Castillo, Sharmba Mitchell, and many more famous names.

The knock against Mayweather is that he picked his opponents carefully and tended to fight the big names when they were on the way down but you can't really criticise his credentials. To go undefeated from 1996 to 2017 while fighting in endless world title fights is pretty amazing whatever way you slice it. When you factor in too that Floyd constantly moved up in weight this makes that achievement all the more incredible.

Mayweather was the consummate boxer. He was punch perfect, had great balance, fast hands, a great jab, and a fantastic defence. Mayweather was the complete package. It's hard to think of a boxer who was more poised and textbook in the ring. In terms of pure boxing IQ, Mayweather was one of the greatest of all time. He was a professor inside the ring. Mayweather could adjust to any opponent and any style and always find a way to win. He could outbox boxers and defuse sluggers.

Mayweather was incredible at super featherweight and made eight defences of the WBC title at that weight. The young super quick Mayweather was an almost perfect fighting machine but he had the savvy and intelligence to be effective too at higher weights as he got older. It's always difficult to place fighters in a historical context and rank them against boxers from other eras but it is probably safe to say that Mayweather would have presented a tricky puzzle to some of the historical greats from 130 to 147 pounds.

You'd probably say that, despite his exploits at multiple weights, Mayweather was at his best in the 130 pound division. Although he wasn't a huge puncher he was very fast and accurate and the accumulation of punches meant that he got a lot of stoppage wins at this weight against some high quality opponents. The weird thing about Mayweather is that although he ended his career as the biggest star in boxing, early on he wasn't considered to be very marketable due to his pure boxing style. It took a long time for Floyd to get the fame and respect that he deserved.

'Prince' Naseem Hamed was born on the first of November, 1974, in the city of Sheffield, England to parents from the Yemen. A prodigy of Brendan Ingle's St Thomas Boxing gym, his talent and flashy southpaw style marked him out from an early age. He entered the pro ranks in 1992 as a flyweight and by 1994 had become the European bantamweight champion, beating the savvy and respected Italian Vincenzo Belcastro with astonishing ease. Hamed appeared to be the most frightening boxing talent to emerge from Britain in many years. His elaborate fight entrances to rap music, cocky assessments of his own talents and brilliant ring performances soon gathered attention. Hamed frequently mocked opponents as he took them apart with punches thrown from gravity defying angles and looked practically unstoppable.

In 1995 he moved up to featherweight and challenged WBO featherweight champion Steve Robinson. Welshman Robinson was an unlikely 'world' champion and had stepped in at late notice to win the WBO belt with a decision over fellow Briton John Davison in April, 1993.. Since then, Robinson had become the 'Cinderella Man'. Spurred on by a boisterous home crowd at the National Ice Rink, Cardiff, the Welshman had made six defences of his title including the high profile scalps of Colin McMillan, Paul Hodkinson and

Duke Mckenzie. Some, including Robinson himself, felt that Hamed would suffer the same fate but on the 30th of September 1995, outdoors at the Cardiff Arms Park, Hamed dominated Robinson with his usual arrogant ease before the battered champion was rescued in the eighth round. Anything seemed possible for 'Naz', the gyrating little genius with dynamite in his gloves.

Hamed's US debut was a wild fourth round knockout of the classy American Kevin Kelley at Madison Square Garden in 1997. Prior to stopping Kelley, Hamed had already beaten IBF champion Tom 'Boom Boom' Johnson in eight rounds in a unification bout and made three knockout defences of his various belts. He was now unquestionably the number one featherweight and appeared to be on the brink of superstardom but 1998 brought only a scrappy win over a faded Wilfredo Vazquez and a dull points decision over the durable but outgunned Wayne McCullough in Atlantic City. More than a few wags were quick to note that Hamed's ring entrances had suddenly become more entertaining than his fights.

A bitter split from lifelong trainer Brendon Ingle and promoter Frank Warren meant that from now onwards Team Hamed would be a family affair. The little known Oscar Suarez was brought in as trainer to replace Brendon Ingle and legendary Kronk wizard Emanuel Steward was hired to join the camp close to fight time. It was a new start for Naz but his first fight in 1999, an alarmingly difficult scrap with fellow Briton Paul Ingle at the M.E.N. Arena, Manchester, suggested a fighter going backwards rather than forwards. Before he rallied to stop the gritty but limited Ingle in the eleventh round, Hamed had appeared dangerously close to running out of gas and suffering a shock defeat. Speculation about his training habits was understandably heightened.

On the 22nd of October of that same year at the Joe Louis Arena, Detroit, Michigan, Hamed seemed to reach a career nadir when he wrestled with Mexican Cesar Soto for twelve tedious and bad-tempered rounds to add the WBC featherweight title to his own WBO belt. A frustrated Hamed was lucky to escape disqualification when he picked Soto up and bodyslammed him to the canvas in the fourth round. He endured the worst headlines of his career but, four months later, seemed to be back on track in London with an impressive fourth round stoppage of the respected former IBF super bantamweight champion Vuyani Bungu.

Hamed entered the ring on a 'flying carpet' and appeared to be back to his cocky best. But the doubts surrounding him resurfaced on the 19th of August, 2000 at the Foxwoods Resort, Connecticut, when he looked shockingly vulnerable and easy to hit against the unheralded Augie 'Kid' Sanchez. Hamed and his connections were criticised for picking Sanchez as an opponent but the underdog put forth a such a game effort he not only decked The Prince but sent him staggering backwards off balance on numerous occasions. Any concerns were masked by the thundering series of punches that put Sanchez away in the fourth round. Despite his technical flaws it still seemed highly doubtful that any featherweight in the world could take what Prince Naseem Hamed would eventually dish out in the course of a fight.

All boxers slowed down a step or two in time but the best ones used the accumulated knowledge of experience to add new skills and tricks. Guile, craftmanship, the ability to slip punches. By contrast, Hamed sometimes gave the impression of a man who had forgotten a little more about his profession each time he stepped back into the squared circle. The precocious bundle of power and flash who evaded punches with instinctive movement and put together dizzying combinations had gradually given way to a more one-dimensional model.

The Prince was increasingly flat-footed as he pawed and probed with his right glove looking to land single bombs. In Hamed's compact 5'3 frame resided uncanny punching power. The Prince wrecked boxers with punches that seemed almost innocuous in the effortless manner of their delivery. He had lost elements of the speed that marked his obstreperous rise to the top but he could still level a medium sized building with either hand. It must have been a reassuring thought as the ragged and untidy elements to his performances became more apparent.

But despite a sterling unbeaten record (35-0, 31 KO's), lucrative television contracts, and a profile and fortune that the rest of the featherweight division could only reflect upon with envy, Hamed still struggled for respect. As far as his critics were concerned he was more hype than substance and more than a few people desperately wanted to see the cocky young upstart humbled in the ring. For as long as anyone could remember the British Muslim boxer had spoken of becoming a legend and winning world championships up to lightweight and beyond. In reality he was marking time against carefully selected opposition as his star gently dimmed.

Suffering from sore hands, struggling to make the weight, and clearly past his best, Hamed lost on points to Marco Antonio Barrera in 2001. Round after round Barrera outboxed Hamed, his calculated strategy making The Prince look inept and confused. Barrera couldn't seem to miss with the left hook and Hamed, in a sure sign he was hurt and confused, mugged and grinned at the Mexican as he was tagged time and again. While The Prince kept his hands low and his chin wide open, Barrera tucked his elbows in and kept his gloves up. He was boxing an incredibly smart and disciplined fight and simply appeared to be in a different class to the man oddsmakers had installed as the favourite. It was a clinical, oddly anti-climatic pounding that saw Hamed in trouble more than once as Barrera blasted him with big combinations.

Hamed only fought once more after the Barrera fight before making a stealth exit from the sport. Despite his reputation as a brash egomaniac, Hamed has been reclusive since retiring from the ring. Could it be that the 'Prince' persona was a character he played - like a super hero alter-ego? In his prime though, circa 1995, Hamed was an awesome fighter. He had fast reflexes and is regarded to be one of the hardest punching featherweights in history. The young Hamed was unquestionably one of the most naturally talented British boxers ever to step in a ring. He was also a great showman and, love him or hate him, the world of boxing has been a bit less colourful ever since those leopardskin trunks left the sport in 2002.

How good was 'The Prince'? While he could realistically claim to have been one of the most successful and innately gifted British boxers of any era, Hamed never met the expectation aroused by the hype that surrounded him, the brashness of his own rhetoric and personality, and, perhaps most of all, the almost unlimited potential he'd once displayed as an emerging fighter in the mid-nineties. His style was based on reflexes and speed and once those had started to slip (for Hamed was never the most dedicated trainer) he had nothing but his punch to fall back on. He was also a 'confidence' fighter. Once he had been demystified by Barrera it was all over.

In his pomp, there was a lot of talk of Hamed moving up to 135 to fight the veteran Azumah Nelson. Hamed sometimes struggled to make featherweight so it seemed like a good idea at the time and Naseem had always talked about winning world titles at multiple weights as if it would be the easiest thing in the world. Talk of a move by Hamed to junior lightweight to pick up another world title petered out though with the emergence of a fresh clutch of young fighters at that weight led by the brilliant Mayweather and the heavy-handed Diego 'Chico' Corrales and Acelino Freitas. Hamed's connections had no desire to put their cash cow in against such opposition for understandable reasons of weight, height and risk. Hamed would have been dwarfed by Corrales and Freitas - who were both huge 130 pounders.

Bob Arum tried to make Mayweather v Hamed but had no joy. Of the Hamed fight, Mayweather said - "Once I got to a certain point [in my career] - very, very quick I wanted to make it happen. He didn't really want to fight. He wanted to be friends. I didn't want to be friends with nobody, I wanted to fight everybody." Hamed, naturally, had a different view. "It's a good job that he didn't fight me though, because he might not have the career that he did," Hamed told BoxingScene.com.

A fight between Mayweather and Hamed was viable from 1998 to 2001 as Floyd was still boxing at super featherweight and so only separated from the Prince by a few pounds. Floyd was so desperate for the fight that he even offered to come in at a catchweight of 128 pounds. The ironic thing is, despite his fame and wealth today, at the time Mayweather needed Hamed much more than Hamed needed him. Hamed had a big HBO contract, could sell out arenas back home in Britain, and was generally seen as much more colourful and marketable than Mayweather. Mayweather was actually considered to be a trifle boring in comparison!

Floyd was therefore desperate for the money and exposure a Hamed fight would bring. Hamed was the bank in the lighter weight divisions. He was the man who generated the revenue. So of course Floyd wanted to fight him and Mayweather was also 100% confident that he would beat Hamed. The American oddsmakers at the time agreed. Mayweather, despite his relative lack of fame ad exposure outside of hardcore boxing circles at the time, would have been the betting favourite had he fought the Prince.

Let us imagine then that Mayweather and Hamed fought in 1999 at a catchweight of 128 pounds. Oddly, both men were fairly inactive and unimpressive when it came to their ring performances in 1999. One can be certain though that they would both be highly motivated and in top condition for this fight. The weight stipulation would favour Hamed (in that Floyd would have to come in below the junior-lightweight weight limit) but Mayweather, at 5'8, was much taller than the 5'3 Hamed.

Both have great reflexes and fast hands. Hamed is by far the bigger puncher but Mayweather is by far the better boxer. Mayweather is textbook and perfect poise. Hamed is completely unorthodox, somewhat clumsy at times, and prone to throwing punches from strange angles (which was actually a strength rather than a weakness). Hamed was a bit like Roy Jones in that he relied on his reflexes to avoid punches rather than block them. This is something which could get him into trouble against a crisp accurate puncher like Floyd.

Hamed had terrible balance but did have good legs though. Hamed was quite stocky and this is clearly what enabled him to punch so hard. He was perfectly capable too of getting on his bike and frustrating an opponent when he wanted to. By the time he fought Barrera, Hamed seemed plodding and stationary and tried to load up on one big punch. The 1999 Hamed though had slightly more left in the tank and hadn't yet regressed that far.

Many people think Mayweather would have stopped Hamed but we have to remember that Hamed had a great chin. The knockdowns Hamed suffered in his career were more down to poor balance than anything. There was never a moment in his career when he seemed in danger of being stopped. Even in the Barrera fight, Hamed never hit the canvas and was never seriously hurt.

Mayweather had a good chin too. More importantly he had a great defence so was incredibly hard to hit. You would have to say that Hamed was easier to hit than Floyd though Naseem wasn't exactly Rocky Balboa in the defence department. Hamed could be very elusive with his head movement and if you went after him you ran the risk of walking onto a big punch. One would expect Floyd, as was his custom, to exercise caution in this fight and be wary of Hamed's power.

Floyd would look to stay out of Hamed's strike zone while still popping the Prince with his own rapier shots. One should remember that Hamed was a switch hitter so he was far from one-dimensional. Hamed had enough speed and mobility to give Floyd more trouble than most fighters did around this time. The general consensus of this fight is that Mayweather, with his better fundamentals and high ring IQ, would have outpointed Hamed and won a clear decision on the cards.

Hamed's great chin would make it very difficult for Floyd to get a stoppage - which wouldn't especially bother Mayweather as a win is a win and he didn't mind how he won he fight so long as he won. The possibility of Hamed landing a Hail Mary can not be completely discounted though. Hamed, at this stage in his career, would ALWAYS land something at some point and he certainly had the power to hurt anyone he hit - even the great Floyd Mayweather.

LARRY HOLMES
V
GEORGE FOREMAN

Although Larry Holmes is generally regarded to be one of the ten greatest heavyweight champions of all time (holding the title from 1978 to 1985), he never really escaped from the illustrious shadow of Muhammad Ali - who he succeeded as champion and once worked for as a sparring partner - and gained a reputation for being a somewhat bitter character who always seemed to have a gripe or complex about something.

Holmes always seemed to resent the fact that he wasn't as loved or appreciated as Ali and his reputation sunk to a low in 1985 when, after building a perfect 48-0 record and on the cusp of drawing level with Rocky Marciano's famous 49-0 mark, he lost a close decision to underdog Michael Spinks and made an infamous and ill-judged comment after the fight about Marciano being unable to carry his jockstrap. Holmes, to put it bluntly, was never one of the most liked heavyweight champions.

Born in Cuthbert, Georgia, into extreme poverty, Holmes didn't learn to read until he was an adult, drifting into small time criminal activities but eventually earning a living through boxing, chiefly as a sparring partner - most famously for Joe Frazier and Muhammad Ali in the early seventies. Frazier hurt Holmes in places he didn't even know he had places in sparring sessions but it was as a sparring partner for Ali at Ali's legendary Deer Lake training camp where Holmes made his name. The young Holmes often held his own with Ali as Ali would never fight flat out in sparring sessions but rather use them to hone a particular strategy he was working on.

In 1980 Holmes and Ali would meet for real in the ring but Holmes was 28 and in his prime while Ali was nearly 40, hadn't fought for two years and had absolutely nothing left. Holmes was admirably honest about his deep reluctance to take this fight and utter dismay at having to batter his idol and mentor. He drew credit for the manner in which he was patently doing his best not to hurt Ali.

Holmes won the WBC heavyweight championship on June 9, 1978, with a 15-round decision over Ken Norton in Las Vegas and defended it an amazing 15 times before a big fall-out with Don King - who more or less controlled the WBC through his close relationship with its president Jose Suliaman. So Holmes adopted the (then) lightly regarded IBF belt and continued to defend as the linear champion until the Spinks upset, though of course not against Don King fighters.

When you consider the longevity of Holmes tenure at the top you begin to understand why he's always felt so unappreciated - even if his resume did include several names that are unlikely to make it into the boxing hall of fame. There were though tough fights against the likes of Shavers, Norton, and Witherspoon. Though people sometimes knock the quality of Holmes' opposition and he DID have a few dud challengers (Lucien Rodriguez and Scott Frank spring to mind), he did beat young undefeated fighters like Tim Witherspoon, Bonecrusher Smith, Carl Williams, and Gerry Cooney. Holmes also beat Mike Weaver - who went on to become the WBA heavyweight champion.

People sometimes say Holmes ducked other fighters in his division like Greg Page, Pinklon Thomas, and Michael Dokes but that seems rather unfair because none of these men, unlike Holmes, could hold onto their titles for very long at all. In all likelihood Holmes would have beaten them all. Holmes is regarded to have one of the greatest jabs in heavyweight history. He also had a sneaky right-hand too and incredible powers of recovery. Holmes was decked by punches from Shavers and Renaldo Snipes that would have levelled buildings but he was somehow able to get up and regain control of the fights.

Holmes' finest hour came when he fought Gerry Cooney in 1982. Cooney, a 6'6 tall white heavyweight contender from New York was unbeaten and a devastating puncher with a record full of brutal knockouts. The handsome and genial Cooney was projected by his eccentric managers Mike Jones and Dennis Rappaport to become the world's first billion dollar athlete if he beat Holmes, becoming a real life Rocky. The fight turns out to be man against boy though as Holmes navigates Cooney's thunderous left-hooks to the body and stops the exhausted challenger in the thirteenth round.

Holmes admitted that the fact that it pitted a white heavyweight against him made it a bigger draw, however depressing this fact might be, and lamented the fact that the carefully matched and frequently inactive Cooney made millions of dollars from boxing because of his skin pigmentation. There was a lot of ill feeling between Holmes and Cooney at the time but they actually became good friends in retirement - which was nice to see.

Boxing was first and foremost a business to Holmes and he made the most of his earning potential, eventually owning a lavish house, a swimming pool shaped like a boxing glove and office complexes in his home town of Easton. He lost again (for only the second time in his long career) to Michael Spinks in a 1986 rematch and, although Holmes was 36 and fading, most still felt he'd done enough to outpoint the younger man. It was the revenge of the boxing establishment says Larry, for his tirades at judges after the first Spinks fight.

Holmes made a comeback in 1988 at the age of 38 to fight the new champion, a young, brutal and apparently unstoppable dynamo called Michael Gerrard Tyson. Holmes admits he was there for the payday and never had enough time to train, getting whacked out by Tyson in the fourth round after making the young sensation look ordinary for a round or two with his experience. Amazingly though, Holmes returned to boxing again in the nineties and even in his forties was still crafty enough to upset hot prospect Ray Mercer and extend Evander Holyfield the full twelve rounds in a 1992 heavyweight title fight. Holmes was also rather unlucky to lose a decision to the WBC champion Oliver McCall. Although it got less exposure and acclaim (the story of Larry's life!), his 1990s comeback was almost as remarkable as the one charted by George Foreman.

As we noted in our previous discussion of Foreman, he was actually due to fight Holmes when they were both 50. The ticket sales were so dreadful though that they scrapped the fight. No one, it seemed, wanted to watch these two old men plodding around the ring. Holmes was actually always quite irritated that George never fought him earlier in the 1990s. Larry felt that he would beat George because George didn't like fighting cagey boxers like himself.

George always preferred to fight punchers and fighters who would come straight at him. There was some truth in this. George DID like to fight aggressive fighters who he wouldn't have to chase. A stylistic nightmare for Old George Foreman early in his comeback would have been someone like Tony Tubbs or Carl Williams. This style of fighter George sensibly avoided. Not to say George wouldn't have beaten these fighters but he definitely didn't like movers or long range boxers. 90s Holmes wasn't much of a mover but he was a very crafty boxer at range when the mood took him. Holmes was the sort of crafty strategic boxer that George disliked fighting.

Anyway, we are certainly not going to speculate on what might have happened had George fought Larry when they were both ancient and at the end of their career. We are going to speculate on what might have happened if George had fought Larry in 1977 or 1978. If George hadn't retired after his loss to Jimmy Young then this fight definitely would have happened sooner or later and probably sooner. George wanted a title shot and Larry wanted a big name opponent. If would have been a natural and obvious fight to make - especially after Larry beat Ken Norton for the WBC title.

Holmes v Foreman, let's say early in 1978, would have been a huge test for the still relatively unknown Larry Holmes and a chance for Foreman to finally get back to the top of the division four years after losing his title to Ali. George was still only 28 at the time and after his up and down fight with Ron Lyle had begun to look more like his old self in wins against Frazier and Scott LeDoux.

The 1970s version of Foreman was more explosive than the 1990s Foreman but he was less relaxed in the ring, more muscle bound, and didn't have the most reliable stamina. If anyone could survive the early rounds against the 1970s Foreman (which, admittedly, was no easy task!) they had a chance at outboxing him because George would begin to get tired. It would probably be fair to say that George, for whatever reason, didn't seem to have boxing in his heart at this point. He only fought four times after the Ali fight and then just walked away (until 1987 at least) from the sport.

The younger version of Foreman didn't seem to crave the limelight and money in the way that the older more gregarious version of George did. Larry Holmes, who had yet to make much money or get any exposure at all, would definitely be the more motivated and desperate of the two regarding this fight. Larry would see George as his coming out party.

George obviously has a big advantage in this fight when it comes to punching power. Make no mistake, George has the ability to hurt Larry in this fight if he can land anything of significance. George was also a good finisher and although he was pretty slow he was surprisingly accurate with his punches.

There's no great mystery about what Larry has to do to win this fight. He simply has to box. Larry will look to get his jab going and stay on the outside. The 1978 version of Larry Holmes had good legs too and was very mobile. Larry certainly has the ability to outbox Foreman and should be able to take the majority of the rounds with his faster hands and good footwork.

The key question here is whether or not George can pressure Larry and turn it into the sort of fight where he can do some real damage. A lot of this will obviously depend on Larry. If Larry's ego and zest for combat gets the better of him and he stands and trades with George then he is only asking for trouble because George is a much bigger puncher. Larry was able to stand flat footed and trade with Ken Norton but he'd be well advised not to do that against George too often.

The best guess in this fight is that Larry, who was peaking and coming into his prime at the time, would find a way to beat George - who wasn't in the best headspace as regards boxing circa 1978. Holmes could well win this fight on points or maybe stop a fatigued Foreman late on. It goes without saying though a man as powerful and indomitable as Foreman can't be ruled out and would be more than capable of springing a (slight) upset with his immense punching power. Larry would have to walk a tightrope and fight a near perfect fight but he certainly had the tools and style to do this. If Jimmy Young could outpoint Foreman at this time you'd have to think that Larry could do the same.